International Appetites for Foreign Equities

Many studies have shown that investors display home bias, that is, they underweight foreign securities in their equity portfolios relative to the prediction of the international capital asset pricing model (ICAPM) that investors should hold the world portfolio (Lewis (1999) and Karolyi and Stulz (2001)). The obvious implication is that one or more assumptions of the ICAPM are unrealistic. Recent studies that attempt to explain home bias have focused on cross-country differences in the availability or cost of information about issuers, in transaction costs, in the liquidity or tradability of securities, and in corporate governance (Ahearne, Griever and Warnock (2004) and Dahlquist, Pinkowitz, Stulz and Williamson (2003) are examples). Particularly striking are findings of much smaller underweights for firms that list on U.S. exchanges using ADRs (Edison and Warnock (2004)). These firms must obey U.S. disclosure and investment protection regulations, and such findings might be interpreted as evidence that investors attribute substantial value to the U.S. regulatory regime.

However, proxy variables for information and transaction costs, liquidity, and corporate governance are imperfect measures. For example, a U.S. ADR listing improves liquidity and reduces transaction costs for U.S. investors, as well as mandating disclosure and governance practices that are familiar to U.S. investors. Moreover, most studies have only examined the portfolios of U.S. investors. The determinants of investment decisions of non-U.S. investors have not been as fully explored, but are crucial to understanding international portfolio positions and capital flows.

We use newly available data to provide evidence about international portfolio investments and their determinants at end-2001 for more than 30 countries, with particular attention to robustness of predictors of portfolio weights across regions and countries. Although many of the most common proxies for information and liquidity costs (such as trade flows, distance, firm size, and beta) are economically and statistically significant in panel regressions that include all sample countries, few if any are robust predictors in subsamples that group countries by region, language, or stage of development. We confirm that U.S. ADR listing status is associated with smaller underweights, but do not find it to be significant outside European and English-speaking countries. In addition, listing on the London Stock Exchange has a similar impact on portfolio weights, especially in Europe.

We present simple summary statistics that help put results in perspective. U.S. equity markets are commonly thought (at least in the United States) to feature more transparency, better governance, greater liquidity, and lower transaction costs than other markets. Strikingly, however, the portfolios of non-U.S. investors underweight U.S. equities to a greater extent than the equities of other regions, usually by a considerable margin. In spite of apparent U.S. advantages, non-U.S. investors in fact are less likely to hold the optimal weight of U.S. equities. This result also carries through to multivariate analysis. The United States also differs from other countries in being relatively distant, in its trade patterns, and in values of other conventional proxies, and these factors taken together explain some of foreign investors' reluctance to hold U.S. equities. However, these factors do not account for all of the underweight in U.S. equities: in our broad cross-country regressions, we find a negative U.S. fixed effect. We interpret our results as consistent with a role for regional preferences or informational advantages that lead foreign investors to weight more heavily close-proximity foreign stocks, and for foreign investors, these advantages more than offset the benefits conferred by U.S. disclosure and governance requirements.

Overall, our results suggest that results based on the portfolio decisions of investors in one or a few nations should be interpreted with caution. Although our results are very consistent with the general implication of the literature that some combination of information, governance, liquidity, and transaction costs are important, our results imply caution in weighting these factors and also suggest that other unmodeled factors may be material. For example, given that a U.K. listing appears about as potent as a U.S. listing, and more so in Europe, the impact of listings on portfolio weights may have more to do with liquidity than with the relative value of regulatory regimes.

Our results also suggest caution in using cross-country equity holdings data. We uncover some large outliers that have a major impact on results. Some outliers are associated with countries that harbor financial centers or that are tax havens, where the measured ultimate ownership of equities may differ from actual ownership. Other outliers appear to be associated with institutional features of individual countries, not with measurement error.

Section 2 reviews a selection of background literature. Section 3 presents the summary statistics and Section 4 lays out our framework of analysis. Section 5 presents regression results and discusses their robustness and economic interpretation, and Section 6 offers concluding remarks.

2. Background Literature

Several factors have been found to be important predictors of how much investors diversify their portfolios internationally and where they invest. The choice between different foreign assets is likely to be influenced by the availability of information about foreign firms, as well as by knowledge about the economic environment in which these firms operate. One would expect that familiarity with the destination country, either through its proximity or through extensive trade links or even political connections (such as those that exist in the European Union) would be among variables that could proxy for information asymmetry. Portes and Rey (1999) utilized a "gravity model" of international trade to analyze bilateral equity flows between 14 countries from 1989 to 1996 and found a role for various information variables. Lane and Milesi-Ferretti (2002) identified growth in goods trade and stock market capitalization as key factors behind international diversification. Their recent work (2003) finds that bilateral equity links are associated with bilateral trade links as well as with more correlated stock returns and output growth rates. They provide evidence that a shared language can be important, as one might expect this to reduce information costs, and document that richer countries with more developed and less volatile markets hold relatively more foreign assets. Using cross-country data on mutual funds' stockholdings, Chan, Covrig, and Ng (2004) find greater home bias in less-developed markets where domestic investors have an informational advantage with respect to local firms. They also find that funds' foreign portfolios are influenced by familiarity, proximity, and market development. Other studies have found that foreign equity investment

2

tends to be skewed towards large firms (Kang and Stulz), for which relatively more information is presumed known. Focusing on U.S. investors' domestic portfolios, Coval and Moskowitz (1999) and Ivkokic and Weisbenner (2003) also find support for location-based asymmetric information. They find that both investment managers and individual investors exhibit strong preferences for investing in locally headquartered firms for which they presumably have an informational advantage.

Dahlquist, Pinkowitz, Stulz, and Williamson (2003) consider the role of corporate governance and concentration in determining investors' portfolios. They document that in countries with poor investor protection, firms tend to controlled by large shareholders so that only a small portion of issued shares are freely traded or "floated", restraining the ability of both domestic and foreign investors to achieve optimal portfolio weights. Aggarwal, Klapper, and Wysocki (2003) find that U.S. mutual funds are more likely to invest in equities of countries with stronger shareholder rights, legal systems, and accounting disclosure. Gompers, Ishii, and Metrick (2001) devise a governance index for 1,500 U.S. firms and find a strong relationship between corporate governance and stock returns. Gugler, Mueller, and Yurtoglu (2003) find that various measures of legal and regulatory protections of investors across many developed and developing countries are important in explaining sources of financing and thus rates of return.

Ahearne, Griever and Warnock's (2004) paper provides evidence that foreign firms reduce information costs by publicly listing securities in the United States. Edison and Warnock (2004) analyzed the importance of cross-border listings and capital controls on capital flows to emerging markets and found evidence that both are important in explaining U.S. investment. They showed that U.S. holdings of emerging market equities tend to be dominated by securities of firms that are large, have fewer restrictions on foreign ownership, and are cross-listed on U.S. exchanges. The firms that cross-list benefit from a lower cost of capital, even though for a destination emerging market, the overall cost of capital falls very little (Bekaert and Harvey (2003)). Karolyi (1998) concludes that stringent disclosure requirements are the main obstacle to listing stocks overseas, which supports the informational role of international listing. Pagano, Röell, and Zechner (2002) document a trend towards listing on U.S. rather than European exchanges. They argue that high-tech and export-oriented European firms listed on U.S. exchanges to take advantage of the deeper and more sophisticated U.S. venture capital market.

3. Summary Statistics

We use newly-released data on foreign portfolio investment from the IMF-sponsored 2001 Coordinated Portfolio Investment Surveys (CPIS) of assets. For the end-2001 asset survey, 65 participating countries ("investors") recorded holdings as of December 2001 of equities and long-term and short-term debt securities issued by firms in approximately 240 destination countries. We focus almost exclusively on equities, leaving the determinants of bond investments to future research. Although 65 countries participated in the CPIS, we limit our examination to 31 of these countries due to limited availability of auxiliary data or for other reasons described below, but these 31 countries account for 86 percent of all foreign equity holdings reported in the coordinated surveys.

We limit our initial sample of *destination* countries to 45, because of difficulties in finding trade, equity returns, and financial market transactions data for many survey destination countries, especially smaller countries. Of the countries that we have to exclude for this reason, the most important in terms of equity held are the major Caribbean and Channel Island financial centers. Because the financial markets as well as many economic statistics of Belgium and Luxembourg are closely integrated and because we speculate that some investor countries were not able to distinguish between their holdings of the two countries, we combine holdings of these two destination countries as one Belgium-Luxembourg destination.[1]

Chart 1 gives a sense of dollar magnitudes, showing the total foreign equity holdings for the 37 investor survey countries with foreign equity holdings of at least $1.1 billion.[2] The United States is by far the largest holder of foreign equities, with investment in December 2001 of over $1.6 trillion. U.S. investors held over $460 billion each in euro area equities and other European equities, about $300 billion in Asian equities and $380 billion in all other foreign equities. The next largest holder of foreign equities is the United Kingdom, with total foreign holdings of $558 billion. After the United Kingdom, the next largest holders are Germany and Luxembourg, each with foreign holdings of more than $300 billion, followed by Switzerland, Italy, the Netherlands, Japan, France, and Canada. Total holdings of foreign equities drop off fairly rapidly after these first ten countries.

However, large dollar amounts of foreign equities do not necessarily imply a well-diversified international portfolio. We define each country X's total equity portfolio as investment by domestic residents in home equities plus investment in foreign equities (from X's asset survey). We then calculate the share of X's portfolio allocated to country Y equities as X's holdings of Y equities divided by X's total equity portfolio:

$$S_x^y = \text{Country X's equity portfolio share in Country Y}$$
$$= \frac{X's\ holdings\ of\ Country\ Y\ equities}{Country\ X's\ total\ equity\ portfolio}$$

Our estimation requires data on home investment in home equities to calculate the portfolio shares. For most countries, we use national account balance sheet data to calculate this portion of the total equity portfolio. For several emerging market countries, these balance sheet data are not available, and instead we use estimates of their total market capitalization in December 2001 from Standard and Poor's Market Factbook. We subtract the reported amounts of their equities held by other CPIS countries as a means of estimating the total amount of domestic equities held

---

[1] For example, the aggregate holding of equities attributed to Luxembourg by all CPIS respondents was $376,010 million, which is considerably larger than Standard and Poor's estimated market capitalization of Luxembourg in December 2001 of $23,883 million.

[2] Throughout this paper "foreign" means from the standpoint of a particular investor country and refers to investments in all destinations besides domestic ones.

by domestic residents.[3] However, we exclude from our set of *investor* countries several CPIS reporters for whom we are unable to construct meaningful portfolio shares: Belgium, Luxembourg, Bermuda, the Bahamas, the Cayman Islands, the Channel Islands, and Ireland. The largest difficulty associated with these major international financial centers is that their reported equity holdings primarily reflect custodial holdings, and we have no means of determining the beneficial owners of equities held in custody in these locations, which makes it essentially impossible to calculate the share of domestic equities held by domestic residents. We also exclude some smaller survey countries because their survey data are extremely sparse, or because we are unable to find trade and domestic asset return data for them.

Chart 2 shows the equity portfolio shares allocated to holdings of U.S. equities, euro-area equities, all other European equities, Asian equities, and all other foreign equities for the 31 countries in our sample; the height of the bar indicates the total share allocated to foreign equities. This chart illustrates that countries that are large holders of equities (as shown in Chart 1) may not be those with the largest shares of their portfolios in foreign equities. We arrange the countries in several regional/cultural groups to draw attention to some common features of portfolios within these groups. Portfolio shares of the Nordic countries are shown at the far left. For these four countries, the share held in foreign equities ranges between 25 percent (for Finland) to over 50 percent (for Norway). For Norway, Denmark, and Sweden, portfolio allocations to U.S., euro-area, and other European equities appear quite similar.

Euro-area country allocations (excluding Finland) are shown in the next set of bars. Although dollar amounts of foreign equities held by investors in the Netherlands were more than six times those held in Austria, foreign equities amounted to about half the equity portfolio in both countries. Foreign equities make up a smaller share of the portfolio–usually between 20 and 25 percent–in most of the remaining euro-area countries, with the exception of Greece, where holdings of foreign securities are only about 2 percent of the portfolio. For most of the euro-area countries, the largest foreign share consists of holdings of equities of other euro-area countries.[4] The share held in U.S. equities is nearly 20 percent in the Netherlands, but is notably smaller in most other euro-area countries. The remainder of euro-area equity portfolios consists primarily of holdings of other European equities (mostly U.K., Swiss, and Nordic equities).

The next set of bars shows allocations for other countries with developed financial markets, arranged into English-speaking and non English-speaking countries. With the exception of the United States, all English-speaking countries have foreign holdings of at least 24 percent of the portfolio. For the United States, the very large foreign equity holdings in dollar

---

[3] We also reconcile financial balance sheet estimates of domestic securities held by foreign residents with estimates of foreign holdings of domestic securities in published International Investment Positions.

[4] One issue is whether one euro area country's investment in equities of another euro area country are more appropriately considered holdings of foreign equities or home equities. Although the euro area has existed as monetary union with a single money market since 1999, euro-area equity markets in 2001 were less than fully integrated. Even in 2003, euro-area equity trading took place primarily on national exchanges, costs for settling equity transactions across borders typically were higher than for purely domestic equity transactions, and differences remained in regulatory and accounting practices. See "The EU Financial Services Action Plan: a Guide," *Bank of England Quarterly Review*, Autumn 2003.

terms translates to less than 12 percent of the total U.S. equity portfolio. For New Zealand, Canada, and Australia, the largest portfolio shares are held in U.S. equities. For non-English speaking countries, the total foreign portfolio share ranges from a high of more than 60 percent (for Switzerland) to a little over 10 percent (for Japan). We suspect Swiss holdings in large part reflect equities held in custody in Switzerland, and the beneficial owners are not necessarily Swiss residents. The large fraction of "Other Foreign" equities indicated by the black section of the Swiss bar primarily reflects substantial holdings classified on the Swiss survey as "Country Unallocated."

The remaining group of countries are those with emerging financial markets. In the group, the Czech Republic has the largest share of foreign equities at nearly 25 percent of the portfolio; the majority of these are "other foreign" equities of Caribbean banking centers. Cyprus has the next largest share; nearly 16 percent of its portfolio is invested in foreign equities. Foreign shares held by the other emerging market countries are quite small.

3.1 Comparing shares with a benchmark market cap portfolio

Following Dalquist, Pinkowitz, Stultz, and Williamson (2003), we adjust for the amount of market capitalization that is actually available to foreign investors by taking account of closely held shares and ownership restrictions.[5] Table 1 compares total market capitalization with this measure of "float-adjusted" market cap. Although U.S. equities made up half of the global market capitalization in December 2001, the share of float-adjusted market cap is somewhat higher at 58 percent. Euro area equities made up the next largest share at just under 13 percent, followed by the United Kingdom at 9 percent and Japan at about 6.5 percent.

The ICAPM has implications not for portfolio shares, but for shares relative to the global market portfolio. To compare each country's investments to the global market portfolio, for each investor country X, we calculate the *relative portfolio weight* of equities held in each destination country Y as the ratio of two fractions: The numerator is the share of each country X's holdings of country Y equities as defined above, and the denominator is the share of country Y's float-adjusted market capitalization (MC) in the global market:

$$W_x^y = \frac{S_x^y}{\dfrac{MC_y}{\sum\limits_{y} MC_y}}$$

If an investor country held 58 percent of its equity portfolio in U.S. equities, for example, this ratio would be equal to 1. For investment in any country Y, a value less than 1 implies an underweight in country Y equities, and a value greater than 1 implies an over-weight position.

We construct a similar measure to determine whether a country's holdings of foreign equities more generally are consistent with the benchmark portfolio. The numerator of this calculation is country X's total foreign equity holdings divided by X's total equity holdings. The

---

[5] Our calculation for float adjustment uses Morgan Stanley Capital International estimates for June 2000.

denominator is the size of the foreign equity market–that is, the global market excluding home equities–relative to the global market:

$$W_x^f = \frac{\displaystyle\sum_{y \neq x} S_x^y}{\dfrac{\displaystyle\sum_{y \neq x} MC_y}{(MC_x + \displaystyle\sum_{y \neq x} MC_y)}}$$

In this case, the weight can also be thought of as a measure of "home bias", as it will be equal to 1 if the share of foreign equities in a country's portfolio equals the share of foreign equities in the global market. A value less than 1 implies an underweight position in foreign equities and a corresponding overweight position in domestic equities (home bias).

Table 2 displays the relative portfolio weights in all foreign equities (column 1), and the weights held in U.S., euro area, U.K., Nordic, Asian, and other industrial country equities (columns 2-7) for our set of investor countries. Rows of the table are grouped in the same manner as bars in Figure 2. Several patterns in the statistics in table 2 are notable. First, the aggregate equity portfolio of every investor country is characterized by home bias (all of the statistics in the first column are less than 1). Although there is variation across the countries in each group, on the whole the bias is least severe for Nordic countries and most pronounced for emerging-market countries. Second, distance appears to matter. For example, the portfolios of most euro-area countries as well as Switzerland overweight equities of other euro-area countries, Nordic countries overweight equities of other Nordic countries, and Australia's weight in New Zealand's portfolio (not shown in the table) is a sizable 4.2. Third, no country's portfolio is less underweight in the U.S. than it is in foreign equities as a whole, and most are substantially more underweight in U.S. equities. Strikingly, in almost every case, the weight of U.S. equities is less than the weight for the "All other" category in which many emerging market destination countries appear.

If, as is commonly argued, U.S. markets are characterized by greater liquidity, lower transactions costs, improved transparency, and corporate governance standards—factors that might be expected to lower the costs of investment in U.S. markets relative to other foreign markets for investors considering cross-border investment—then one might expect that U.S. equities would be *more* highly weighted in foreign investor portfolios than are equities of other foreign countries. In terms of the Cooper-Kaplanis (1985) model of international portfolio allocation, if the cost to investing in the United States is small relative to costs for investing in other countries, then U.S. equities should be held closer to their market capitalization weights than are equities of other foreign countries. In our analysis below, we explore the extent to which proxies for these factors account for foreign portfolio allocations, the extent to which other features of the United States such as its distance from other countries work to discourage ownership of U.S. equities, and the extent to which other factors encourage holdings of non-U.S. equities in foreign portfolios.

Our calculation of portfolio shares also helps identify a number of "outliers" in the raw survey data.[6] Because we compare equity shares in the domestic portfolio with shares in market capitalization, we can easily see when reported holdings are surprisingly large relative to market capitalizations, because the calculated portfolio weight in that country will be very large. For example, reported holdings of Colombian equities in the Netherlands survey are over $5 billion, which amounts to essentially the entire float-adjusted market capitalization of Colombia. The associated Netherlands portfolio weight in Colombia is an extraordinarily large 49.0 compared with an average Netherlands portfolio weight of 0.5. Moreover, we note that in the newly-released 2002 CPIS survey for the Netherlands, reported holdings of Colombian equities is 0. We suspect that the 2001 data are in error, and treat the Colombia observation for the Netherlands as an investor country as a missing value. Examination of the data also reveal considerable overweight in Russia by Cypriot investors: Russian equities account for over half of Cypriot foreign equity holdings, resulting in a portfolio overweight of 76.7.[7] We find other large, though not as glaring, overweights in other destination countries for several investor countries. As we note below, we include destination country fixed-effect dummy variables in our estimation to capture some of these investments, but we find that we can only attain satisfactory model performance by dropping Russia as a destination in our emerging-market sample.

Table 3 lists the fraction of reported foreign equity holdings for each country that we end up including in our destination sample, along with the primary reason for incomplete coverage. For Nordic and euro-area countries, our sample is fairly complete, as we are able to include about 97-98 percent of total reported foreign holdings; the residual is holdings by excluded destination countries. For English-speaking countries, coverage is slightly less. For the United States, we are able to include about 88 percent of the reported equity holdings, with holdings of equities in Caribbean financial centers the primary exclusion. For Switzerland and Hong Kong, we are able to include only about 75 percent and a bit under 60 percent, respectively. For these countries, a major reason for exclusion is confidential or "unallocated" data included in the country's total equity holdings but not reported against any destination country. Coverage is also notably sparser for several of our emerging market countries, in large part reflecting either

---

[6] Our calculation of portfolio weights and subsequent identification of data outliers suggests that the CPIS data should be used with caution. As noted in the individual country metadata for the CPIS surveys, countries used a variety of techniques to determine securities holdings. Some surveys are conducted using end investors, some using custodians responding on behalf of clients, and some use a combination of the two. In countries that survey primarily end-investors (such as Canada and the United Kingdom), holdings of foreign securities by the household sector and by non-financial corporations may be missed. In countries that survey primarily resident custodians (such as Germany and Switzerland), securities entrusted to non-resident custodians may be missed. Countries also differ in their ability to cross-check responses with other sources of information on cross-border holdings (for example, with regulatory sources or with Balance of Payments transactions data). Finally, of the 31 countries we consider, only 12 required respondents to report on a security-by-security basis. This technique is generally considered to be the most accurate, as it enables data collectors to better cross-check responses for accuracy of country of residence of the issuer of each security and of the market value of the security, and helps avoid possible double-counting of securities that may be reported by both an end-investor and a custodian.

[7] This overweight in Russian equities most likely reflects Cyprus's status in 2001 as a offshore financial center that was especially attractive to Eastern European and former Soviet Union countries. See for example the IMF report "Cyprus: Assessment of the Offshore Financial Sector," July 2001.

holdings in financial centers or because confidential location data were suppressed in the survey. For Cyprus, once Russia is excluded as a destination country, the destination sample coverage falls to less than 50 percent.[8]

We exclude Austria as an investor country from most of our analysis because we find that Austrian portfolio allocations are markedly different from those in other countries in our sample, with notably large investment in eastern European countries. Whereas Austrian foreign equity holdings account for less than 1 percent of all survey country foreign equity holdings, they account for 11 percent of all Hungarian equities, nearly 15 percent of Polish equities, and nearly 37 percent of Czech Republic equities. These large eastern-European investments amount to considerable Austrian portfolio overweight in these countries: the Austrian portfolio weight is 17.2 in Polish equities, 23.4 in Hungarian equities, and 70.2 in Czech equities. In contrast, German weights in these countries are only 0.1, 0.4, and 0.2, respectively.[9]

4.0   Framework of analysis and proxy variables

Our empirical analysis is motivated by the theoretical model of Martin and Rey (1999) (see Appendix 1 for a derivation that extends to multiple countries and is expressed in terms of portfolio weights). Our estimation equation in practice is similar to that specified by Ahearne, Griever, and Warnock, in which portfolio weights are determined in part by differential costs of investing across investor-destination country pairs.[10] These costs depend on various frictions such as restrictions to foreign investment, transaction costs or custodial fees, the costs of acquiring information, and the legal environment. We explore how several measures of differential costs help explain overweight or underweight positions in international equity portfolios.

The dependent variable is the relative float-adjusted portfolio weight of each destination country Y's equities for each investor country X (W_x^y) as of December 2001 (as defined above). Explanatory variables for these weights include measures of trade, distance between investor and destination countries, measures of a market beta investment in each destination country, the amount of shares that are cross-listed on investors' own exchanges (when available), measures of financial market depth and tradability, transactions or information costs, market concentration, and accounting disclosure. Some of these variables are specific to each investor-

---

[8] The exclusion of the major financial centers from our sample as investor countries raises the question of whether U.S. equities are held more heavily in these locations, and whether the global underweight in U.S. equities that we observe would be ameliorated by inclusion of these countries. This does not appear to be the case. Only for the Bahamas are U.S. equities more than half the reported foreign holdings. Taking the results for all 65 survey countries together and excluding the U.S., only $1 trillion out of roughly $3.5 trillion in total equities is held in U.S. equities.

[9] We speculate that the high portfolio weights in these countries in part reflects the growing expansion of Austrian banks into the financial services industry in Eastern Europe.

[10] Although Aheane et al base their estimation equation on the model of Cooper and Kaplanis (1985), the basic implications of our framework and their model are the same: investors should weight more heavily those equities for which they have better information or for which transactions are lower.

destination county pair while others apply more generally across all investor countries. We estimate our model as a panel, allowing for investor country fixed-effects and correcting for heterogeneity, and include dummy variables for destination country fixed-effects as well.[11] The motivation for each variable and its construction is as follows:

Variables specific to each investor-destination country pair

Trade connections (TRADE):

Investors may have a greater proclivity to hold securities of close trading partners for a variety of reasons, including hedging, familiarity with destination country products and their producers, or spillovers of information. We use the direction of trade statistics from the International Monetary Fund to calculate total bilateral trade (exports + imports) between each investor country and each destination country in 2001 relative to each investor country's total exports + imports. We expect more trade to be associated with larger portfolio weights.[12]

Distance between country capitals (DISTANCE and DISTSQR):

We also include the distance between country capitals (measured in thousands of miles) which may proxy for information or settlement costs, as well as other factors such as culture and language for which country proximity may be a proxy. Although technological advances have lowered the effect of distance on information costs substantially in recent years, investors may still be more prone to underweight equities in countries that are far away and thus perhaps physically unfamiliar to them. We allow for a non-linear relationship by including both distance and distance squared. Our hypothesis is that investors are more likely to underweight equities of countries that are farther away.

Measures of Market Return (BETA):

Especially if transaction or information costs or other frictions make holding the world portfolio suboptimal, correlations of investor and destination country returns may influence portfolio allocations. We include an estimate of the beta between each investor-destination country pair.[13] We expect this variable to enter with a negative sign.

---

[11] While we allow for investor country fixed effects in all of our analysis below, we include only those destination country fixed effects that are statistically significant.

[12] We also experimented with an alternative measure of total trade scaled by home country GDP, but generally this variable is not as significant.

[13] We calculate each investor country/destination country beta as the slope coefficient from a regression of the monthly percent change in the investor country MSCI equity price index on the monthly percent change in the MSCI equity price index for each destination country, expressed in currency of the investor country, over the previous three years. Our choice of the domestic country stock return rather than a global index return as the basis of comparison is driven by the extent of home bias evident in our investor country samples. We believe that most of these investors consider the possibility of investing abroad compared with returns in their home market. We find that our results are robust to an alternative specification of BETA which substitutes the MSCI global index return for the domestic country return.

Cross-listed equity (XLIST)

Investors may prefer investing in foreign equities that are cross-listed on their home stock exchanges because cross-listing may lower information and transactions costs, and may also signal adherence to domestic accounting standards. For several investor countries, we are able to calculate the percentage of each destination country's market capitalization that is represented by foreign firms cross-listed on the domestic exchange; we expect a positive contribution in these cases.

Common Language (LANGUAGE)

Common language may also reduce information costs for investors because they are better able to read company financial reports and financial press analysis if they are written in a shared language. Common language may proxy for factors such as colonial ties, which may enhance knowledge of or familiarity with the financial system in the investor country. For each investor-destination country pair, we include a dummy variable capturing whether they share a common national or official language; we expect a positive contribution from this variable.

More general variables

U.S. ADR (USADR)

Foreign equity offered as American Depository Receipts (ADRs) is more likely to be held by U.S. investors, presumably because they lower transactions and information costs for U.S. investors. In addition, issuance as a level 2 or 3 ADR is also interpreted as a way to signal a firm's intent to adhere to U.S. accounting standards, which are presumed to be more stringent than those in other nations (Ahearne, Griever, and Warnock 2004). To see whether foreign investors are similarly attracted to equities offered as ADRs (and thus perhaps to U.S. accounting standards), we include the percentage of each destination country market capitalization represented by firms included in the Bank of New York's (BoNY) ADR index as of December 2001. We assume that all U.S. equities held by foreigners are exchange-listed and thus satisfy these same disclosure and accounting standards, and so the value of the ADR variable for the U.S. as a destination country is 100.[14] We expect this variable to have a positive sign.

---

[14] This choice implies that if the USADR variable enters significantly, U.S. equities should get a proportional boost in foreign portfolios because, by definition, 100 percent of U.S. market captialization is listed on U.S. exchanges, compared with an average of about 20 percent of foreign market capitalization offered in the form of USADRs. The alternative is to specify the value of USADR for the U.S. as a destination country as 0, implying that only *foreign* equity satisfying U.S. listing requirements receives an additional benefit from being listed on a U.S. exchange. When we used this alternative specification, we tended to find a significant coefficient on USADR. Note that a positive coefficient in this case actually implies that–all other factors equal–U.S. equities are relatively disfavored in foreign portfolios, because the contribution from this variable is 0 for the United States as a portfolio destination.

Listing on the London Stock Exchange (UKLSE)

Because London is a major European financial center, listing on the London stock exchange may give a comparable benefit in terms of exposure, access, and signaling of adherence to international standards. We include a variable similar to USADR that instead includes the percentage of foreign market capitalization that is listed on the London exchange.[15]

Firm Concentration (FIRMCON)

If a foreign equity market is dominated by the shares of a few well-known large companies, the "name recognition factor" may result in foreign investors holding a relatively larger proportion of that country's equities. We include as an explanatory variable the fraction of each destination country's market capitalization that is attributable to the largest 10 firms in the country, and expect the variable to enter with a positive sign.

Measures of market depth (MCAPGDP, EQTYBOND)

We expect that foreign investors may be more likely to hold equities of countries with more developed capital markets. These markets may have greater liquidity and lower transactions costs beyond what we are able to control for with our measure of equity transactions costs noted below. To capture these effects, we include as an explanatory variable the market capitalization of equity of firms in each destination country relative to its GDP (MCAPGDP) as a measure of the relative size and importance of equity finance in the destination country. We also include the ratio of equity market capitalization to bond market capitalization in each destination country (EQTYBOND). If equities are relatively more prevalent than bonds in a given country, foreign investors wishing to achieve an internationally balanced portfolio may be more likely to hold equities of that country. We expect portfolio weights to be positively related to these measures.

Transactions costs (EQTCOST):

Higher transactions costs may discourage equity holdings in some destination countries. We include the Elkins-McSherry estimates of the costs (in basis points) of purchasing equities on various international exchanges as of 2001, including commissions, fees, and "market impact," the difference between the price at which a trade is executed and the average of the stock's high, low, opening, and closing prices on that trading day.

Measures of Accounting Disclosure (ACCOUNT)

---

[15] Although the correlation between USADR and UKLSE is fairly high (.75), a firm-by-firm comparison of UKLSE listings with BoNY ADR constituents indicates that relatively few firms are both listed on the UKLSE and have equities issued as ADRs. Our UKLSE variable is constructed similarly to the USADR variable, with a value of 100 for the United Kingdom as a destination country.

Surveys indicate that investors care about accounting standards and disclosure in making portfolio choices. A 2002 McKinsey survey found that a majority of the more than 200 institutional investors surveyed put corporate governance issues as equally important to or more important than financial issues in evaluating companies to invest in.[16] Following Ahearne, Griever, and Warnock (2004) and Aggarwal, Klapper, and Wysocki (2003), we include a measure of accounting disclosure developed in LaPorta et al (1998) as a proxy for the importance of the regulatory regime and accounting standards in determining portfolio allocations.

Additional variables considered

As noted by Edison and Warnock (2004), some developing countries place restrictions on foreign ownership of equities in particular industries. We computed the ratio of investable market capitalization relative to total market capitalization for each destination country. However, we found this variable to be insignificant in all our specifications, and do not report results including this variable in part because it is available for only a limited number of destination countries and thus reduces our sample size. We also considered the log of GDP per capita as an indicator for financial development, but found this variable to be insignificant in all of our specifications as well.

Table 4 lists the mean values for dependant and explanatory variables for all the investor countries and subsets we consider in our sample. The full sample average values (column 1) obscure some important regional differences, especially in bilateral investor-destination country variables. Subsequent columns show regional means for Nordic countries, euro area countries (excluding Finland), English-speaking and other developed countries, and emerging market countries. In addition, we list the average values for Nordic investment in other Nordic countries (column 3) and for intra-euro area investment (column 5).

As shown in the first row, the average float-adjusted portfolio weight for Nordic countries is .65 (column 2), but this average obscures the considerable overweight of 2.69 in other Nordic countries. Trade with other Nordic countries makes up a larger fraction of total trade in each Nordic country (over 6 percent) than does trade on average, and the distances between Nordic countries are relatively short. About 31 percent of Nordic equity is issued as U.S. ADRs, and 32 percent is listed on the London Stock exchange, and a larger fraction of other Nordic equity is cross-listed on Nordic exchanges (about 9 percent) than is equity in general (.7 percent).

Although the average foreign portfolio weight for euro-area countries is quite high (.6), this reflects in part an overweight in holdings of other euro-area equities (1.94). Intra-euro-area trade is a notably larger share of total euro-area trade (over 5 percent on average) and on average euro-area countries are closer together than they are to other countries. A greater portion of euro-area equity is issued as ADRs (44 percent) and listed on the London Stock Exchange (30 percent) than is true for all destination countries, but for the countries where we have the data,

---

[16] McKinsey and Company: Global Investor Opinion Survey: Key Findings, July 2002.

relatively little euro-area equity is cross-listed on domestic exchanges (2 percent).

5.0   Main regression results:

Table 5 lists the results from our basic sample of 30 investor countries, excluding Austria as an investor country and also excluding Russia as destination countries. In model 1A (column 1), the distance variables and BETA enter significantly at the 1 percent level (denoted by **). The size of the distance coefficients imply a sizable difference in portfolio weight from being 1,000 miles apart compared with being 5,000 miles apart: the extra distance reduces the portfolio weight by about .6. The coefficient on BETA indicates a relatively modest impact for country investor-destination country pairs with BETAs close to 1 and a more significant negative impact for country pairs with very large values of BETA.

USADR enters positively, but with an insignificant coefficient, as do FIRMCON and EQTYBOND. However, the coefficient for listing on the London exchange, UKLSE, enters significantly at the 5 percent level in the alternative specification in model1B. TRADE enters significantly at the 10 percent level in models 1A and 1B but with larger coefficients and at the 1 percent level in 1C and 1D where we omit the distance variables. This suggests that some of the impact we capture with the distance variables may reflect knowledge about a given country's firms brought about by trade. In model 1C, USADR remains insignificant, but FIRMCON enters very significantly. In model 1D, both UKLSE and FIRMCON are significant. Thus, our explorations in these initial cross-country models suggests that while listing on the U.K. stock exchange does appear to enhance foreign ownership, a U.S. ADR listing does not have a comparable effect for foreign investors in general.[17] One caveat is that half of our investor country sample is made up of European countries, and it may be that for European investors, London listing is especially important. We explore this possibility more fully in our country subsample regressions below.

Models 1E and 1F introduce the LANGUAGE variable to models 1A and 1B. LANGUAGE enters with a sizable, significant coefficient (just under .8 in both specifications) but reduces the size and significance of the coefficient on TRADE and, to a lesser extent, the coefficient on distance. This again suggests that some of the contribution from trade and from proximity may reflect lower information costs which are also captured through common language. However, apart from an increase in the (negative) contribution from MCAPGDP, introducing the language variable has little additional effect on the size or significance of other explanatory variables, and gives only a modest increase in overall model fit. The impact of LANGUAGE is most important in explaining English-speaking investor country portfolio weights in English-speaking destination countries. Countries that share English as a common or

---

[17] In alternative specifications not reported, we substituted listing on the New York stock exchange for the USADR variable. We found no significant differences from including this alternate variable. We also experimented including both USADR and UKLSE. We found these results to be very similar to 1B.

national language are, on average, relatively far apart from one another, and models 1A and 1B tend to underestimate the portfolio weights in these country pairs.[18]

Coefficients on destination country dummies also are reported in Table 5. The large positive and significant dummy variable for Belgium-Luxembourg in all these models indicates the extent to which financial centers (and associated problems of attribution) may influence measured foreign portfolio holdings, over and above what can be accounted for by trade links, market depth, stock price comovement, or measures of market access or information.

The bottom row of coefficients in the table reports the coefficient on the dummy variable for the United States. In all specifications—both those using the USADR variable (1A, 1C, and 1E) and those using the alternative UKLSE variable (1B, 1D, and 1E)—the U.S. dummy variable enters with a significant negative sign; this dummy variable ranges in size from -.31 to -.63. These results suggest that U.S. equities are in fact relatively *disfavored* in foreign investor portfolios, even when accounting for the relatively large physical distance of the United States from other countries, and even accounting for differences in foreign listing, market concentration, and the relative importance of trade with the U.S. In results not reported, we did not find accounting disclosure or transactions costs variables to be significant, either entered individually or together.[19]

Models 1G and 1H add the measure of foreign equity cross-listed on domestic exchanges, XLIST, for the countries where we have this data.[20] Including this variable reduces the sample size to 13 investor countries, and excludes all emerging-market investor countries. We find no evidence that cross-listing has a significant effect on foreign portfolio allocations in general, although the subsample excludes two economies that have a substantial number of listed foreign firms, Germany and Hong Kong. USADR does enter significantly in this sample. However, we find also that UKLSE enters significantly when substituted in model 1F. This finding suggests caution in interpretation of the ADR finding in cross-country comparisons: for non-U.S. investors, the benefit to issuance as an ADR (or to listing on the London exchange) may have more to do with the liquidity of the U.S. and U.K. markets and the information aspects of either U.S. or U.K. listing than a preference for adherence to U.S. accounting standards. In this smaller sample, TRADE enters significantly at the five percent level even in the presence of the distance variables, and BETA remains significant. Finally, the U.S. destination dummy variable is significant and negative in both specifications, indicating that the relative underweight in U.S.

---

[18] On average, the total effect on the estimated portfolio weight for these countries is somewhat smaller than the net effect of the common language, trade, and distance variables, because the estimated fixed-effect constant terms for English-speaking investor countries are also somewhat smaller than in models 1A and 1B.

[19] Including either of these variables reduces our sample size as data are missing for several of our destination countries.

[20] Australia, Denmark, Finland, France. Italy, Japan, Netherlands, Norway, New Zealand, Sweden, Switzerland, the United Kingdom, and the United States.

equities is more than can be accounted for by trade links, distance, market returns, and international listing.[21]

In model 1I, we reproduce model 1A using the full sample that includes all 31 investor countries and all 46 destinations. Overall fit of the model is notably weaker, with an adjusted R^2 of .10. Apart from some significant destination dummies, the only variables that are significant with the expected signs are BETA and the distance variables. MCAPGDP enters significantly but with a negative sign. In this specification, the U.S. dummy variable enters with an insignificant positive sign, but we do not interpret this result as indicating a preference for U.S. equities because it is completely offset by the *negative* contribution from the USADR variable in this case.

We find evidence of significant investor country fixed effects in all of our full-sample models, as noted by the likelihood ratio Chi-square and F-test values in the last rows of the tables. Table 5A lists the estimated fixed-effect constant terms for each investor country from model 1A, and, for comparison, for 1E which includes the language dummy variable. Most of these coefficients are close to 1, but range from .54 for Greece to 2.2 for Singapore. The size of these country-specific slope coefficients helps put the (negative) contributions from distance into perspective: on average, countries are 7,500 miles apart, and in model 1A this distance would reduce the typical country weight by about 1: about offsetting the intercept contribution. Although test statistics favor the fixed-effect model over the classic regression model, the improvement in fit is relatively minor: the adjusted R^2 from the single-specification alternative is .202, compared with .217 in the fixed-effect model.

5.1   Robustness

Taken together, the results suggest that the significance for foreign investors of the U.S. and U.K. listing variables along with firm concentration may have more to do with market liquidity or "name recognition" than signaling a preference for equities that adhere to higher U.S. or "Anglo-Saxon" accounting standards. Moreover, the commonly presumed desirability of the U.S. as a destination for investment because of its large, liquid market and its corporate governance and shareholder protection standards does not appear to be enough to overcome other U.S. characteristics that apparently make it a relatively less desirable destination in the eyes of investors in many nations. Factors such as distance or trade connections also appear to matter, suggesting further support for the importance of information about a given country's firms for portfolio allocations. However, we also find considerable unexplained variation, as indicated by the low adjusted R^2. This led us investigate whether the "one-size fits all" fixed-country effect estimation captures all the factors explaining different countries' equity portfolios. We look at five "regional" or market-type specifications: Nordic countries (including Finland),

---

[21] The larger coefficient on the U.S. destination dummy in model 1E than 1F offsets the larger positive contribution from the 100 percent U.S. listing in the USADR variable in 1E.

euro-area countries (excluding Finland), English-speaking advanced economies, other countries with advanced financial markets, and countries with emerging financial markets.[22]

Nordic Countries

Table 6, models 2A and 2B, shows results for the four Nordic countries (Denmark, Finland, Norway, and Sweden). Model 2A includes the USADR variable and 2B substitutes UKLSE. Because we are able to construct XLIST for all of the Nordic countries, we include this variable in both specifications. Results are generally similar to those of the all-country regressions, although we find that trade but not distance matters for Nordic portfolios, and in contrast to models 1E and 1F, XLIST enters significantly with a coefficient that suggests an even larger effect than from listing in London: cross-listing 20 percent of the market capitalization on the Nordic home exchange increases the average Nordic portfolio weight by .43, whereas the same fraction listed in London increases the weight by .12. FIRMCON also enters significantly in both 2A and 2B, but if FIRMCON is excluded, USADR enters significantly with a coefficient about equal to that of the coefficient of UKLSE in 2B. These results confirm the overlap in these variables and support the interpretation that they capture aspects of liquidity and "name recognition."[23]

Even after controlling for trade, betas, and the various measures of foreign listing, significant destination fixed effects are captured by the dummy variables for DENMARK, FINLAND, NORWAY, and SWEDEN. These variables show that the Nordic destination overweight apparent in table 2 is not uniform: it is notably and significantly larger for Sweden (3.7) and DENMARK (2.2) than for FINLAND (.3) or NORWAY (.8). A possible explanation for the size and significance of these variables is that Nordic investors exhibit a Covar-Moskowitz style regional preference: for Nordic investors, the relative costs to investing in other Nordic equities are likely to be quite small compared with the costs of cross-border investment more generally, perhaps because of familiarity with or preference for Nordic firms not captured by our standard measures of proximity and trade connections.

The U.S. dummy variable is a significant -.32 in 2A (when USADR is included) but is small and insignificant in 2B when UKLSE is used instead. The difference in these coefficients reflects the smaller percentage of U.S. market capitalization listed in London: the larger negative coefficient on the US destination dummy variable in 2A offsets the larger positive contribution from U.S. capitalization in USADR. Taking all the variables in 2B together, the results indicate

---

[22] To a large extent, our choice of country groups is determined by observations from chart 2 and tables 2 and 3 and priors regarding cultural similarities across country groups. However, experimentation suggests that our results are little affected by the inclusion of any given country in the groupings we present. For instance, although we include Finland in the Nordic group, the results we present below are little affected if instead we include Finland with other euro-area countries.

[23] In results not reported, we find little evidence that the measures of accounting disclosure, transaction costs, or capital controls matter for Nordic portfolios. We also exclude the common language variable from the Nordic regressions, because the only Nordic country pair that shares LANGUAGE are Finland and Sweden. These two countries also have the greatest extent of cross-listing, and including both variables in the Nordic subgroup makes it difficult to disentangle the actual contributions of each.

that, compared with equities from other *non*-Nordic countries, U.S. equities are neither especially favored nor disfavored in Nordic portfolios, and the relative portfolio weight in U.S. equities can be explained by factors such as trade and betas, and to some extent, listing of U.S. equities on a major international exchange.

Euro area countries:

Models 3A-3B report our results for euro-area countries, using a euro-area sample that excludes both Austria as an investor country and Colombia as a destination country, for the reasons outlined above.[24] Our preferred euro-area model specifications are similar to our Nordic specifications, with 3A including USADR and 3B substituting UKLSE, except that we exclude XLIST, as we do not have this information for many euro-area countries, and we include a euro-area destination dummy variable instead of Nordic dummies.[25]

Both USADR and UKLSE are significant, and suggest similar effects on euro-area portfolios as we found for UKLSE on Nordic portfolios: issuing 20 percent of the market capitalization of a given country as an ADR or on the London exchange would increase the average euro-area portfolio weight in that country by about .12. FIRMCON enters significantly in model 3B but not in 3A when USADR is included, again suggesting some overlap in the three variables, and again supporting the interpretation that these variables are capturing information associated with liquidity and recognition.[26]

In contrast to the all-country and Nordic regressions, neither TRADE nor distance enters significantly in either specification. However, both the euro-area destination dummy variable and the Belgium-Luxembourg dummy variables are significant, and given the extent of intra-euro-area trade, these variables may be proxying for information or familiarity brought about by proximity, trade connections, and other regional information advantages. The size of the coefficient on Belgium-Luxembourg (around 11) raises concern that some of these reported holdings may reflect custody holdings in Belgium or Luxembourg that are in fact equities issued by firms in other countries. Models 3C and 3D exclude Belgium-Luxembourg as a destination. Overall model fit deteriorates to an adjusted R^2 of .23, but the significance of FIRMCON and BETA are improved. In all four euro-area models, the euro-area dummy ranges between .36 and .47, smaller than several of the Nordic dummy variables in 2A and 2B. This suggests that although equity portfolios of euro-area countries are heavily weighted and in some cases somewhat overweight in holdings of equities of other euro-area countries—for example, the French portfolio weight in German equities is .75; in Italian equities is .8; and in Dutch equities

---

[24] Results for Austria are reported in Appendix 2.

[25] In results not reported, common language was not significant in explaining euro-area portfolios.

[26] The correlation between UKLSE and FIRMCON is larger than for USADR and FIRMCON: .415 compared with .263. If all three variables are included, USADR and UKLSE both enter with significance at the 10 percent level, but FIRMCON is no longer significant, and the coefficient on UKLSE is larger than that on USADR. In unreported regressions, neither accounting disclosure, nor transaction costs, nor capital controls matter for euro-area portfolios. In addition, we do not find significance for our measure of cross-listing for the three countries in this euro-area sample (France, Italy, and the Netherlands) for which we have been able to construct the XLIST variable.

is 1.65—a fair amount of the portfolio allocation to euro-area equities can be explained by stock price co-movements, foreign listings, and market concentration.

As with the Nordic regressions 2A and 2B, we find significant negative coefficients on the U.S. destination dummy variable in 3A and 3C (the specifications including USADR), and insignificant coefficients in 3B and 3D (when UKLSE is substituted). As with our Nordic regressions, we interpret these results as suggesting that euro-area equities are favored in euro-area portfolios, while U.S. equities are neither especially favored nor disfavored compared with other non-euro equities. Although U.S. listing as captured by the USADR variable helps explain euro-area portfolio allocations, this benefit applies to equities of all countries that list on U.S. exchanges, and U.S. equities are not favored proportionally to the amount listed.

Other developed economies:
English-speaking countries

We also find roles for market liquidity and familiarity or "name recognition" in the portfolio allocations of English-speaking countries (the United States, Canada, the United Kingdom, Australia, and New Zealand, shown in Table 7, Models 4A-4D).[27] Both USADR (4A) and UKLSE (4B) help explain portfolio weights, and FIRMCON also enters significantly in both specifications. In contrast to our findings for other regions, the measure of accounting disclosure, ACCOUNT, is significant in explaining English-speaking portfolios in Model 4C. The finding for ACCOUNT confirms results found by Aggarwal, Klapper, and Wysocki and others of the importance of this variable when looking at U.S. portfolios, but our results suggest a note of caution in its interpretation. The significance may have more to do with familiarity with accounting practices than an assessment of standards. The Nordic overweight identified in the Nordic regressions 2A and 2B (and the insignificance of ACCOUNT in the Nordic regressions) may reflect in part familiarity with or preference for Nordic accounting and disclosure practices that is not readily transferable to other countries with similar high numeric ratings. Euro-area investors' preference for other euro-area equities–which generally have a somewhat lower disclosure rating according to the ACCOUNT variable–may reflect in part a preference for a familiar European system of accounting.[28]

Model 4D includes XLIST for the subset of the United States, the United Kingdom, Australia, and New Zealand. We do not find any additional significance from cross-listing on the

---

[27] Although we had found LANGUAGE to be significant in our all-country models 1E and 1F with the largest effect for English-speaking countries, we did not find LANGUAGE to be significant when included in the these regressions for the subset of English-speaking countries. We expect this is because the contribution of LANGUAGE offset some of the effect from the distance variables for these countries in models 1E and 1F; neither LANGUAGE nor distance are significant when included for the English-speaking investor countries.

[28] Indeed, the McKinsey Global Investor Opinion Survey 2002 found that while 90 percent of investors surveyed agreed that a single accounting standard would be desirable, they disagreed on which standard they would prefer to see adopted. North American investors favored the GAAP over the IAS by a margin of 76 percent to 24 percent, but Western European investors preferred the IAS over GAAP 78 percent to 22 percent.

home exchange once USADR is included.[29] The other major difference from models 4A-4C is that TRADE enters significantly in this specification, suggesting a role for familiarity with a country's firms brought about by trade connections. We expect that this result is largely because Canada is excluded from this sample. The United States makes up a disproportionate share in Canadian trade (76 percent), but Canadian portfolios are not likewise disproportionally weighted in U.S. equities.[30]

In all four English-speaking models, the US dummy variable enters with a sizable negative coefficient, but it is significant at the 10 percent level only in models 4A and 4D. On balance, we interpret these results as suggesting that U.S. equities are in fact somewhat unfavored for these countries: although table 2 indicates that U.S. equities are about evenly weighted with all foreign equities in the portfolios of these countries, the model results suggest that given the extent of trade with the United States, the importance of foreign listing, and familiarity with "Anglo-Saxon" accounting standards, U.S. equities should be *more* heavily weighted.

Other countries with advanced financial markets and countries with emerging financial markets

Our next estimation samples include the remaining countries with developed financial markets (Table 7, Models 5A and 5B)[31] and emerging market countries (Model 6)[32]. For both sets of countries, the only significant variables other than specific destination country dummy variables are the distance variables, providing further support for a role for information or familiarity with a country's firms brought about by proximity. The coefficient on US is positive but insignificant in model 5A and positive and significant at the 5 percent level in model 6; in both cases the positive contribution from this coefficient is more than offset by a large negative contribution from distance: on average, these countries are quite far from the United States (nearly 12,000 miles for the other developed countries, and about 9,500 miles for the emerging market countries). 5B lists results when the distance variables are excluded for the developed countries. In this specification TRADE gains significance, but overall model fit deteriorates.[33] The coefficient on US in 5B is a significant -1.29, just about offsetting the average positive contribution from trade with the U.S. Taken together, the results indicate a preference for

---

[29] We do not interpret the insignificance of XLIST in the English-speaking sample as contrary to previous research that has found cross-listing in the United States to be significant in explaining U.S. investor portfolios, because USADR and the U.S. XLIST variable are highly correlated. Our analysis uses only published aggregate data for all countries, whereas Ahearne, Griever, and Warnock explore this issue on a security-by-security basis for U.S. data and thus can explore the effects of cross-listing and ADR issuance independently.

[30] In an alternative regression where we include Canada as an investor country but exclude the United States as a destination country, TRADE again enters significantly with a coefficient similar in size to that in 4D.

[31] Japan, Hong Kong, Singapore, South Africa, and Switzerland.

[32] Brazil, Chile, Cyprus, Czech Republic, Egypt, Greece, Hungary, Israel, S. Korea, and Malaysia.

[33] UKLSE does not enter significantly if it is substituted for USADR in either 5A or 5B. We included XLIST in separate regressions for Japan and Switzerland, the only two of these countries where we have been able to construct this variable, but it does not enter significantly and model fit is not otherwise improved.

equities of countries that are closer to the investor country or with whom trade ties are relatively strong. The size, signs, and significance of the US destination dummy variables suggest that the U.S. is not a favored destination for investors in either set of countries, but neither is it as disfavored as its distance from these countries would indicate.

5.2   Economic significance and interpretation

To put the results of all these estimated models into perspective, table 8 compares the relative contributions of the variables that are most commonly significant across regional groups: trade, distance, issuance as an ADR or listing on the London Stock Exchange, cross-listing on the domestic exchange, firm concentration, and Beta. Significant coefficients and contributions are highlighted in bold.

Trade and Distance:

In the regression results for all countries, both trade and distance are significant in determining portfolio shares, indicating a role for familiarity or country preference brought about by trade or proximity. As trade is (inversely) correlated with distance, we also calculate the combined effect of being relatively close to the destination country (500 miles) and having a relatively high trade share with that country (10), compared with being relatively distant (7,500 miles) and having a trade share of only 2. Results from the all-country models 1A, 1B, and 1E demonstrate the considerable impact that trade and distance together have on portfolio shares: being further away with a smaller trade share reduces the predicted share for a country by nearly 1 in all three models. When distance is suppressed (models 1C and 1D), the effect from trade alone is increased, but it is still only about half as large as the combined effects: an increase in trade share from 2 to 10 raises the predicted weight by about 0.5. In these two models, however, the contribution from FIRMCON is much larger than in models 1A, 1B, and 1E, suggesting again that some of the effect we capture through distance may reflect familiarity or "name recognition" that is not adequately captured by trade shares.

Trade or distance were also significant for many of the country subsamples, although the combined effects vary in size across specifications. For English speaking countries excluding Canada (Model 4D), the increase in trade share raises the estimated portfolio weight from .12 to .61. Roughly similar effects are found for trade alone in other developed economies (Model 5B) and for distance in emerging market economies (Model 6). The effect of distance for non-English speaking countries with developed financial markets (Model 5A) was especially large, but these distance results should be considered in connection with the estimated fixed-effect intercepts for these countries, which range from 3.2 for Japan to 4.4 for Singapore.[34] For Nordic countries (Models 2A and 2B), the effect from an increase in trade share is a bit smaller than for all countries: between .2 and .3., and neither trade nor distance were significant in the euro-area regressions. However, in both the Nordic and euro-area regressions, destination dummies for

---

[34] Thus, on net, these results generate relatively high weights for equities of destination countries that are close to these investor countries, but much lower weights for countries that are more distant.

other Nordic and other euro-area countries entered with sizable and highly significant coefficients. The importance of these destination countries–which are both close in proximity to and have high trade shares with the respective investor countries–suggest that the role of information brought about by familiarity is likely at work for these countries as well.

USADR and UKLSE:

Listing on the London Stock Exchange has remarkably consistent effects across most developed market country groups. An increase in a country's market capitalization cross-listed in London from 0 percent to 40 percent increases the estimated portfolio weight of that country by between .28 and .32 when estimated over all countries (models 1B and 1D), by .24 for Nordic countries, and by .28 for euro area countries (models 3B and 3D). Effects for English-speaking countries are somewhat smaller (.11, model 4B). The same increase in market capitalization issued as an ADR generally has somewhat smaller and less uniformly significant effects. The greater significance of London listing over US ADR issuance for many European investor countries cautions against interpreting the findings on USADR (when significant) as indicating a strong preference for U.S. corporate governance. We also note that U.S. listing does not imply any additional benefit for U.S. equities, as they are not especially favored in foreign portfolios. Instead, our results suggest that the benefits of listing on a major international exchange may be the increased liquidity and easier access offered by London or U.S. listing.

Cross-listing on the domestic exchange:

Our results for cross-listing were somewhat surprising in that this variable was significant in fewer cases than we had expected, perhaps in part because of the relatively small amount of foreign equity listed on European exchanges, as noted by Pagano et al. For Nordic countries, cross-listing is significant, with a larger potential impact than either ADR issuance or listing on the London exchange. Listing 40 percent of a country's market capitalization on Nordic exchanges raises Nordic portfolio weights in that country by between .85 and .88 (Models 2A and 2B), more than three times the comparable impact from either USADR or UKLSE.[35]

Firm concentration:

The percentage of market capitalization accounted for by the top ten firms in a country also has a significant effect on country portfolio weights in Nordic, euro-area, and English speaking portfolio allocations. As we note above, the contribution from FIRMCON is enhanced in some specifications that exclude distance, and there also appears to be an overlap with the contributions from London and U.S. listing. These results suggest an important role for "name recognition" in foreign portfolio allocations. For Nordic countries, an increase in FIRMCON

---

[35] One concern is relatively few foreign firms are listed on Nordic exchanges, and of those that are listed, many are other Nordic firms. However, any Nordic-centric bias is likely to be picked up by the specific Nordic destination dummy variables in these regressions, so we have more confidence that the cross-listing variable is picking up the effects of listing of non-Nordic firms.

from .2 to .6 increases estimated the portfolio weight in that country from about .15 to over .5 (Models 2A and 2B). The effect is smaller for euro-area countries in Model 3A (from about .06 to a little over .2). The increase for English-speaking countries is similar to that of the euro area (models 4A-4D). In general, these increases are about as large as from an increase in percentage of market capitalization listed on the London exchange from 0 to 40 percent.

Betas

In contrast to the sizable estimated effects found for trade, distance, and foreign listing, our results for BETA suggest fairly minimal effects on portfolio weights if betas fall in a narrow range, as is true for most advanced economy investor-destination country pairs. Even a beta of 15 reduces the estimated portfolio weight by less than .1 in most instances. The significance of this variable is likely picking up more extreme effects from some developing market destination countries with considerably higher estimated betas.

6.0   Conclusions

Our empirical analysis of the determinants of the equity portfolio allocations of thirty one countries in December 2001 yielded several interesting results. In particular, we were surprised by the finding that virtually all countries we examine underweight U.S. equities more than they do foreign equities in general, in some cases by a substantial margin. Factors such as market liquidity, corporate governance, and accounting standards have been found to matter for U.S. investment in foreign equities, and previous research has found that U.S. investors are more likely to hold foreign equity that is cross-listed on a U.S. exchange or offered as an ADR, as such offering not only lowers information and transactions costs but also signals adherence to U.S. accounting standards. However, our study indicates that such features of the U.S. market do not give U.S. equities any particular edge in foreign portfolios.

We found country and regional fixed effects to be important determinants of the degree of portfolio diversification. Nordic countries appear overweight in equities of other Nordic countries to an extent beyond what can be explained by trade shares and foreign cross-listings and by standard proxies for market liquidity, transactions costs, common language, and accounting disclosure. Likewise, euro-area countries and Switzerland appear to overweight equities of other euro area-countries. These results suggest some role for locational or regional preferences such as Coval and Moskowitz find for U.S. investors, perhaps capturing unmeasured informational advantages about nearby firms. Once these regional preferences are accounted for, U.S. equities do not appear to be disproportionally disfavored in their portfolios. At the same time, though, U.S. equities are not especially favored, and in other regional specifications we find stronger evidence that U.S. equities are underweighted to a greater degree than our model determinants can explain.

Our work confirms some findings in the literature that previously have been documented primarily for the United States. We find that cross-listing equities on foreign exchanges adds some explanatory power at least for some investor-destination pairs. Issuing U.S. ADRs or listing on the London stock exchange appear to be more generally significant factors, but in part this result may reflect the much larger amount of foreign market capitalization listed on the U.S.

and U.K. exchanges than on most foreign exchanges we considered. Our finding that including firm concentration at times reduces the size and significance of the coefficients on USADR and UKLSE suggests that these variables may be capturing some "name recognition" effect that helps reduce information costs. Information variables seem to be crucial. Even though equities issued or listed in the United States are considered to be superior on disclosure, accounting rules, and governance, this does not appear to overcome perceived or actual information advantages that attract non-U.S. investors to other "nearby" markets.

References

Aggarwal, R., L. Klapper, and P. Wysocki, 2003. Portfolio Preferences of Foreign Institutional Investors, Working Paper, 2003.

Ahearne, A., W. Griever, and F. Warnock, 2004. Information costs and home bias: an analysis of U.S. holdings of foreign equities. *Journal of International Economics.*

Bakaert, G. and C. Harvey, 2003. Emerging market finance. *Journal of Empirical Finance.*

Chan, K., V. Covrig, and L. Ng, 2004. What determines the domestic bias and foreign bias? Evidence from mutual fund equity allocations worldwide. Forthcoming in *Journal of Finance.*

Cooper, I. and E. Kaplanis, 1986. Costs to crossborder investment and international equity market equilibrium, in Edwards, J., Franks, J., Mayer, C. And Schaefer, S. (Eds), *Recent Developments in Corporate Finance*, Cambridge University Press: Cambridge.

Coval, J. and T. Moskowitz, 1999. Home Bias at Home: Local Equity Preference in Domestic Portfolios. *Journal of Finance.*

Dahlquist, M. and G. Robertsson, 2001. Direct foreign ownership, institutional investors, and firm characteristics. *Journal of Financial Economics,* 59:413-440.

Dahlquist, M., L. Pinkowitz, R. Stulz, and R. Williamson, (2003). Corporate governance and the home bias. *Journal of Financial and Quantitative Analysis*, 38:87-110.

Edison, H. J., and F. Warnock, 2004. U.S. investors' emerging market equity portfolios: a security level analysis. Forthcoming in *Review of Economics and Statistics* (June).

Faruqee, H., S. Li, and I. Yan (2004). The determinants of international portfolio holdings and home bias. IMF Working Paper 04/34.

Gompers, P., J. Ishii and A. Metrick, 2001. Corporate governance and equity prices. National Bureau of Economic Research Working Paper no. 8449.

Gugler, K., D. Mueller and B. Yurtoglu, 2003. The impact of corporate governance on investment returns in developed and developing countries. *Economic Journal*, 113:F511-F539.

Ivkovic, Z. and S. Weisbenner, 2003. Local Does as Local Is: Information Content of the Geography of Individual Investors' Common Stock Investments. National Bureau of Economic Research Working Paper no. 9685.

Kang, J. and R. Stulz, 1997. Why is there a home bias? An analysis of foreign portfolio equity ownership in Japan. *Journal of Financial Economics,* 46:3-28

Karolyi, G.A. 1998. "Why Do Companies List Shares Abroad?: A Survey of the Evidence and Its Managerial Implications." *Financial Markets, Institutions and Instruments* 7 (1): 1–60.

Karolyi, G.A. and R. Stulz, 2002. Are financial assets priced locally or globally? National Bureau of Economic Research Working Paper no. 8994.

Lane, P. R. and G. M. Milesi-Ferretti, 2002. International Financial Integration.

Lane, P. R. and G. M. Milesi-Ferretti, 2003. International Investment Patterns.

LaPorta, R., Lopez-de-Silanes, F., Shliefer, A., and Vishny, R. Law and finance. *Journal of Political Economy*, 106: 1115-1155.

Lewis, K., 1999. Trying to explain the home bias in equities and consumption. *Journal of Economic Literature,* 37:571-608.

Mann, C. L. and E. E. Meade, 2002. Home Bias, Transactions Costs, and Prospects for the Euro: A More Detailed Analysis. Centre for Economic Performance Discussion Paper 0537.

Martin, P. and H. Rey (2004), "Financial Super-Markets: Size Matters for Asset Trade," *Journal of International Economics,* forthcoming.

Obstfeld, M., and K. Rogoff, 2000. The six major puzzles in international macroeconomics: Is there a common cause? National Bureau of Economic Research Working Paper no. 7777.

Pagano, M., Roell, A., and J. Zechner, (2002) The geography of equity listing: Why do companies list abroad? *Journal of Finance* 57 no. 6.

Portes, R., and H. Rey, 1999. The determinants of cross-border equity flows. National Bureau of Economic Research Working Paper no. 7336.

Solnik, B. H., 1984. Why not diversify internationally rather than domestically? *Financial Analysts Journal,* 30:48-54.

Stulz, R. M., 1984. Pricing capital assets in an international setting: An introduction. *Journal of International Business Studies* 15:55-73.

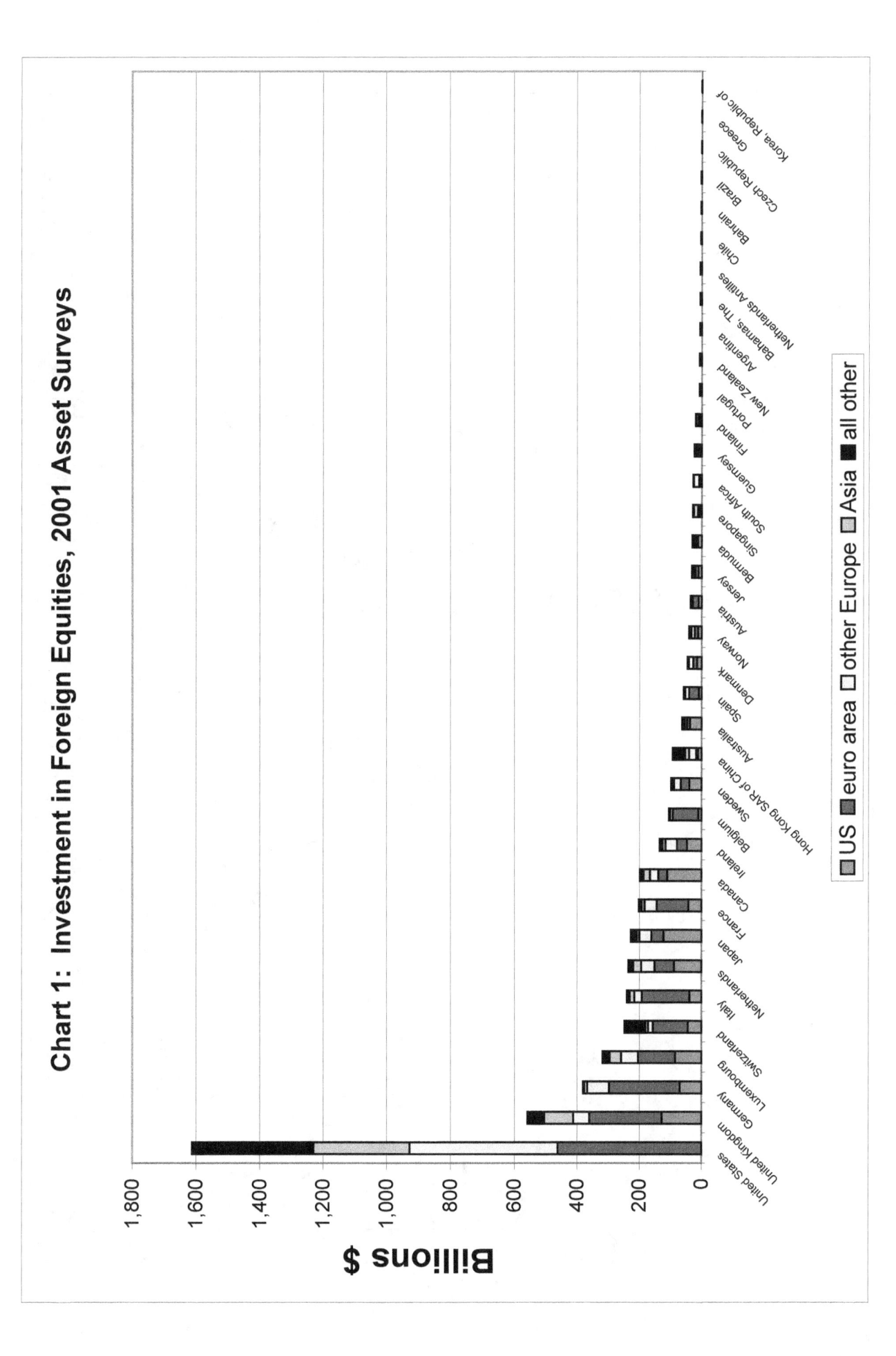

Chart 1: Investment in Foreign Equities, 2001 Asset Surveys

Chart 2

Equity Portfolio Allocations

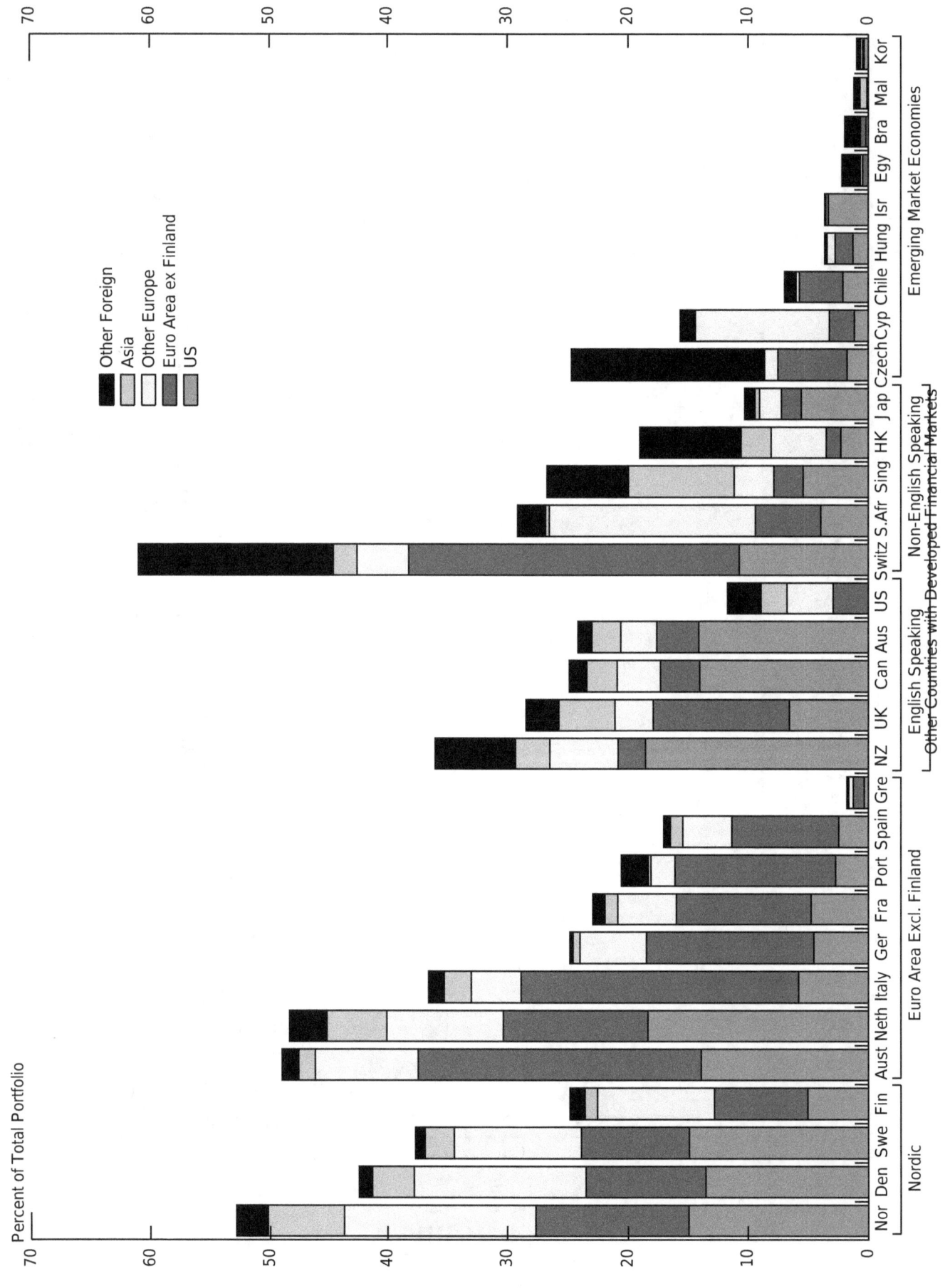

Source: 2001 Coordinated Asset Surveys and National Financial Balance Sheet Accounts

Table 1. Market Capitalization and Float-Adjusted Market Capitalization

	S&P Market Capitalization Dec. 2001	Estimated percent float*	Float-adjusted market capitalization	Share of Global Float-Adjusted Market Cap
United States	13,810,429	94	12,981,803	58.2
Euro area	4,237,466	67	2,854,520	12.8
United Kingdom	2,217,324	92	2,039,938	9.1
Japan	2,251,814	65	1,463,679	6.6
Other Asia	2,108,768	41	868,342	3.9
Other Industrial	1,232,549	80	982,966	4.4
Other Europe	1,045,823	75	788,950	3.5
All Other	881,695	39	342,109	1.5
Total	27,785,868	80	22,322,308	100.0

* MSCI estimates of the percent of "free-float" market capitalization controlling
for ownership restrictions and closely-held shares, as of June 2000

Table 2: Float-Adjusted Relative Portfolio Weigts for Individual Investor Countries

	total foreign weight (1)	U.S. (2)	Euro Area (3)	Nordic (4)	UK (5)	Asia (6)	All other (7)
Nordic Countries:							
Norway	0.53	0.26	1.04	2.78	0.97	0.63	0.56
Denmark	0.43	0.23	0.81	2.98	0.71	0.34	0.45
Sweden	0.38	0.26	0.73	1.98	0.64	0.24	0.37
Finland	0.25	0.09	0.63	4.52	0.29	0.10	0.31
Euro area (excluding Finland)							
Netherlands	0.49	0.32	1.13	0.75	0.66	0.50	0.66
Austria	0.49	0.24	1.93	0.40	0.40	0.14	0.69
Italy	0.37	0.10	2.10	0.33	0.27	0.22	0.28
Germany	0.26	0.08	1.51	0.55	0.32	0.06	0.21
France	0.24	0.08	1.26	0.38	0.32	0.11	0.27
Portugal	0.21	0.05	1.09	0.16	0.14	0.02	0.33
Spain	0.17	0.04	0.84	0.24	0.34	0.10	0.13
Greece	0.02	0.01	0.07	0.01	0.03	0.00	0.02
Other developed: English speaking							
New Zealand	0.36	0.32	0.19	0.25	0.52	0.28	0.87
United Kingdom	0.31	0.11	0.92	0.80	--	0.45	0.52
United States	0.28	--	0.24	0.32	0.28	0.21	0.41
Canada	0.26	0.24	0.27	0.25	0.28	0.25	0.37
Australia	0.24	0.24	0.29	0.17	0.24	0.23	0.23
Other developed: non-English speaking							
Switzerland	0.62	0.18	2.24	0.63	0.33	0.20	2.70
South Africa	0.29	0.07	0.44	0.10	1.83	0.03	0.32
Hong Kong	0.19	0.04	0.10	0.00	0.50	0.27	1.03
Singapore	0.27	0.09	0.20	0.08	0.33	0.89	0.84
Japan	0.11	0.10	0.13	0.10	0.15	0.10	0.14
Emerging Markets:							
Czech Republic	0.25	0.03	0.47	0.07	0.05	0.00	2.03
Cyprus	0.16	0.02	0.17	1.09	0.03	0.01	1.20
Chile	0.07	0.04	0.30	0.08	0.01	0.01	0.10
Israel	0.04	0.06	0.02	0.00	0.00	0.00	0.01
Hungary	0.04	0.02	0.12	0.01	0.04	0.01	0.05
Egypt	0.02	0.00	0.04	0.00	0.02	0.00	0.19
Brazil	0.02	0.00	0.04	0.00	0.00	0.00	0.17
Malaysia	0.01	0.00	0.00	0.00	0.00	0.06	0.06
S. Korea	0.01	0.01	0.01	0.00	0.00	0.02	0.04
memo: share in float-adjusted market cap		**58.16**	**12.28**	**2.07**	**9.14**	**10.20**	**8.16**

Float adjustments: Estimates from Morgan Stanley Capital International for June 2000. See "MSCI Consultation Paper on Free Float-Adjusting Constituent Weights and Increasing the Target Market Representation in its Indices", mimeo, September 17, 2000, available at http://www.msci.com.

Table 3: Percent of Foreign Equity Holdings Included in Destination Sample

	Percent of reported foreign equity holdings included in estimation sample	Primary exclusions and omissions
Nordic Countries:		
Norway	97.96	
Denmark	99.62	
Sweden	99.13	
Finland	95.24	
Euro area (excluding Finland)		
Netherlands	95.96	Colombia (would be 98.1 percent with Colombia included)
Austria	98.00	
Italy	98.62	
Germany	99.42	
France	96.84	
Portugal	93.02	Financial centers and unallocated or confidential data
Spain	98.89	
Greece	92.53	Unallocated or confidential data
Other developed: English speaking		
New Zealand	97.39	
United Kingdom	93.50	Financial centers and unallocated or confidential data
United States	88.40	Financial centers
Canada	96.73	
Australia	97.03	
Other developed: non-English speaking		
Switzerland	75.25	Financial centers and unallocated or confidential data
South Africa	92.86	Financial centers and unallocated or confidential data
Hong Kong	58.27	Financial centers and unallocated or confidential data
Singapore	90.85	Financial centers
Japan	94.56	Financial centers
Emerging Markets:		
Czech Republic	34.68	Financial centers
Cyprus	45.25	Russia (would be 97.2 percent with Russia included)
Chile	90.71	Financial centers
Israel	98.87	
Hungary	98.23	
Egypt	30.95	Unallocated or confidential data and international organizations
Brazil	41.92	Financial centers
Malaysia	61.19	Financial centers and unallocated or confidential data
S. Korea	78.59	Financial centers and unallocated or confidential data

Table 4. Mean Values of Dependent and Explanatory Variables, by Country Group

		All Countries	Nordic		Euro Area*		English-Speaking Countries	Other Developed Countries	Emerging Market Countries
			All Destination countries	Nordic Destination Countries	All Destination countries	Euro Area Destination Countries			
Float-Adjusted Portfolio Weight (dependent variable)		0.46	0.65	2.69	0.57	1.94	0.28	0.68	0.25
Explanatory Variables:									
TRADE	as share of total trade	2.18	2.18	6.14	2.08	5.18	2.36	2.29	1.95
MCAPGDP	ratio of market cap to GDP	0.72	0.70	0.83	0.70	0.60	0.68	0.68	0.71
EQTYBOND	ratio of market cap to bond market	1.63	1.67	0.97	1.68	0.72	1.65	1.62	1.60
DIST	Distance between country capitals, in thousands of miles	7.64	5.79	0.58	6.00	1.50	9.86	8.62	7.60
USADR	Percent of destination country's equity market cap issued as ADRs	24.54	23.61	31.36	23.21	44.31	23.46	24.04	24.28
UKLSE	Percent of destination country's equity market cap listed on the London Stock Exchange	16.15	15.82	32.12	15.99	29.78	16.00	16.14	15.97
XLIST	Percent of destination country's market cap cross-listed on investor country exchange**	3.89	0.69	9.22	0.48	2.03	9.36	3.78	n.a.
FIRMCON	Ratio of destination country market cap of top 10 firms to total destination country market cap	0.49	0.48	0.66	0.48	0.62	0.49	0.48	0.48
BETA	Slope coefficient from regression of destination country mothly stock return on investor country stock return	1.48	1.62	0.80	2.67	0.75	2.05	1.88	0.58
ACCOUNT	Accounting disclosure index	62.97	62.39	74.00	62.81	60.57	62.42	62.50	62.70
LANGUAGE	Shares common official or national language	0.10	0.01	0.17	0.05	0.06	0.22	0.17	0.05

* Excluding Finland; Finland included in Nordic group
** Mean value of countries in group where data is available

Table 5: Results from models with all investor countries

	1A	1B	1C	1D	1E	1F	1G	1H	1I[1]
TRADETOT	0.018 +	0.020 +	0.051 **	0.053 **	0.014	0.016	0.041 *	0.044 *	0.005
MCAPGDP	-0.052	-0.092 *	-0.124 **	-0.168 **	-0.124 **	-0.159 **	0.007	-0.030	-0.246 *
EQTYBOND	0.016	0.021	0.011	0.018	0.019	0.023 +	0.004	0.006	0.010
DIST	-0.190 **	-0.189 **			-0.179 **	-0.179 **	-0.111 *	-0.103 *	-0.349 **
DISTSQR	0.007 **	0.007 **			0.007 **	0.007 **	0.004	0.004	0.014 **
USADR	0.002		0.001		0.002		0.005 *		-0.001
UKLSE		0.008 *		0.008 *		0.007 *		0.007 *	
XLIST							0.005	0.004	
FIRMCON	0.157	0.040	0.715 **	0.533 **	0.222	0.110	0.272	0.269	0.637 +
BETA	-0.007 **	-0.009 **	-0.003	-0.004 +	-0.006 *	-0.007 **	-0.005 *	-0.007 *	-0.028 **
LANGUAGE					0.781 *	0.765 *			
EURO	-0.171 +	-0.247 *	0.028	-0.108	-0.125	-0.200 *	-0.185	-0.186 +	-0.574 *
BELUX	5.129 **	5.267 **	5.106 **	5.332 **	5.037 **	5.173 **	7.588 *	7.609 *	5.211 **
UK	-0.331 +	-0.946 **	0.192 +	-0.558 +	-0.325 +	-0.885 **	-0.476 +	-0.926 *	-0.317
MALAYSIA	1.098 *	1.137 *	1.045 +	1.109 *	1.221 *	1.257 *	0.108	0.110	1.076 *
SINGAPORE	0.271 **	0.365 **	0.015	0.156	0.149	0.241	0.286 +	0.305 +	0.110
NORDIC	-0.097	-0.183	0.089	-0.012	-0.016	-0.095	0.246	0.179	-0.530 *
US	-0.408 *	-0.313 *	-0.572 **	-0.629 **	-0.390 *	-0.328 *	-0.806 **	-0.505 *	0.121
N	1285	1285	1287	1287	1285	1285	556	556	1359
Adjusted R^2	0.2166	0.2191	0.1961	0.1994	0.2274	0.2283	0.2817	0.2825	0.0979
Mean of dependent variable	0.4541	0.4541	0.4534	0.4534	0.4541	0.4541	0.5826	0.5826	0.596
Tests for significance of investor country fixed effects:									
Chi-square	51.908 **	51.935 **	59.649 **	59.848 **	46.108 *	46.316 *	13.776	13.867	52.056 **
F	1.763 **	1.764 **	2.035 **	2.042 **	1.561 *	1.568 *	1.102	1.109	1.709 *

** significant at 1 percent
* significant at 5 percent
+ significant at 10 percent

[1] Estimated over full sample including Austria and outlier destination countries

Table 5A: Estimated investor country fixed effect constant terms from selected all countries models

	Model 1A			Model 1E*		
	Coefficient	Standard Error	t-ratio	Coefficient	Standard Error	t-ratio
Australia	1.05	0.394	2.67	0.84	0.397	2.12
Canada	0.96	0.378	2.56	0.71	0.383	1.84
Denmark	1.13	0.339	3.34	1.11	0.337	3.30
Finland	0.94	0.341	2.75	0.90	0.339	2.65
France	0.92	0.337	2.73	0.84	0.336	2.51
Germany	1.10	0.336	3.28	1.03	0.335	3.07
Greece	0.55	0.345	1.59	0.52	0.343	1.53
Hong Kong	0.92	0.373	2.46	0.70	0.376	1.86
Italy	1.80	0.339	5.30	1.75	0.337	5.21
Japan	0.86	0.382	2.26	0.82	0.380	2.17
Korea	0.75	0.374	2.02	0.72	0.372	1.93
Netherlands	1.09	0.338	3.22	1.04	0.336	3.11
New Zealand	1.05	0.389	2.71	0.83	0.394	2.10
Norway	1.33	0.340	3.92	1.31	0.338	3.88
Portugal	1.17	0.347	3.37	1.12	0.345	3.26
South Africa	1.37	0.399	3.44	1.16	0.400	2.89
Spain	0.83	0.344	2.42	0.70	0.344	2.03
Sweden	1.04	0.340	3.05	1.00	0.338	2.95
Switzerland	1.74	0.337	5.15	1.60	0.338	4.74
United Kingdom	1.08	0.338	3.18	0.88	0.342	2.58
United States	1.01	0.380	2.67	0.81	0.381	2.12
Brazil	0.88	0.385	2.29	0.82	0.382	2.15
Chile	1.21	0.393	3.08	1.05	0.393	2.67
Cyprus	1.13	0.345	3.29	0.89	0.353	2.54
Czech Republic	1.02	0.337	3.02	1.00	0.336	2.98
Egypt	0.57	0.350	1.64	0.54	0.347	1.57
Hungary	0.68	0.337	2.01	0.66	0.335	1.96
Israel	0.67	0.353	1.91	0.65	0.351	1.84
Malaysia	0.85	0.375	2.28	0.82	0.373	2.20
Singapore	2.17	0.376	5.78	1.91	0.383	4.98

* Includes dummy variable for common language

Table 6: Results for Nordic and euro area country samples

	Nordic		Euro Area		Euro area: excludes Belgium-Lux.	
	2A	2B	3A	3B	3C	3D
TRADETOT	0.032 **	0.018 **	-0.013	-0.012	0.007	0.008
MCAPGDP	-0.044	-0.079	0.011	-0.037	0.000	-0.049
EQTYBOND	-0.023 **	-0.019	0.008	0.010	0.008	0.011
USADR	0.003		0.006 **		0.005 *	
UKLSE		0.006 +		0.007 *		0.007 *
XLIST	0.021 *	0.022 *				
FIRMCON	0.860 **	0.855 **	0.272	0.336 +	0.360 **	0.413 **
BETA	-0.006	-0.009 *	-0.002	-0.004 +	-0.002 *	-0.003 *
EURO			0.439 *	0.468 *	0.364 **	0.377 *
BELUX	4.370 **	4.429 **	11.846 **	11.803 **		
DENMARK	2.178 *	2.196 *				
FINLAND	0.437 +	0.297				
NORWAY	0.766 **	0.783 **				
SWEDEN	3.687 **	3.717 **				
US	-0.320 *	-0.036	-0.404 *	0.066	-0.425 **	-0.009
N	174	174	300	300	293	293
Adjusted R^2	0.7091	0.7181	0.536	0.5375	0.2296	0.2527
Mean of dependent variable	0.6467	0.6467	0.5789	0.5789	0.2971	0.2971
Tests for significance of investor country fixed effects:						
Chi-square	9.422 *	10.262 *	14.136 *	13.989 *	28.117 **	29.008 **
F	2.912 *	3.179 *	2.284 *	2.259 *	4.667 **	4.822 **

** significant at 1 percent
* significant at 5 percent
+ significant at 10 percent

Table 7: Results for English-speaking, other developed country, and emerging market country samples

| | English-Speaking Countries | | | | Other developed | | Emerging Markets |
	4A	4B	4C	4D	5A	5B	6
TRADETOT	0.025	0.025	0.024	0.061 *	-0.015	0.088 *	-0.001
MCAPGDP	0.004	-0.014	-0.137 *	-0.176 *	0.005	-0.128	-0.172 *
EQTYBOND	-0.001	-0.001	0.040	0.047 +	0.007	0.040	0.016
DISTANCE				0.001	-0.659 *		-0.100 *
DIST SQR				0.001 **	0.026 *		0.004 *
USADR	0.002 **		0.002 *	0.001 **	0.002	0.001	-0.002
UKLSE		0.003 **					
XLIST				0.002			
FIRMCON	0.387 **	0.420 **	0.391 **	0.471 **	0.105	0.623	0.346
BETA	-0.002	-0.003 *	-0.002	-0.002	-0.005	0.008	-0.006
ACCOUNT			0.007 **	0.005 +			
BELUX	0.050	0.036	0.051	0.070	8.167	8.208	1.625 +
SINGAPORE	0.354 **	0.350 **	0.300 **	0.352 **	-0.088	0.041	0.085
MALAYSIA							2.760
US	-0.857 +	-0.670	-0.743	-0.782 +	0.330	-1.290 *	0.424 *
N	220	220	180	144	220	220	343
Adjusted R^2	0.3168	0.3176	0.2937	0.4210	0.2264	0.1441	0.1660
Mean of dependent variable	0.2941	0.2941	0.3043	0.3231	0.6814	0.6814	0.2481
Tests for significance of investor country fixed effects:							
Chi-square	57.027 **	53.489 **	39.237 **	36.916 **	7.142	8.330 +	12.626 +
F	6.773 **	14.175 **	10.047 **	12.566 **	1.691	1.987 +	1.725

Excludes Canada

** significant at 1 percent
* significant at 5 percent
+ significant at 10 percent

Table 8: Comparison of Effects of Key Variables Across Country Samples

Model:	All countries						Nordic		Euro Area				English-Speaking				Other Developed		Emerging Markets
	1A	1B	1C	1D	1E	1G	2A	2B	3A	3B	3C	3D	4A	4B	4C	4D	5A	5B	6
Trade																			
model coefficient	0.018	0.020	**0.051**	**0.053**	0.014	**0.041**	**0.032**	0.018	-0.013	-0.012	0.007	0.008	0.025	0.025	0.025	**0.061**	-0.015	**0.088**	-0.001
effect from increase in trade share:																			
2	0.04	0.04	**0.10**	**0.11**	0.03	**0.08**	**0.06**	0.04	-0.03	-0.02	0.01	0.02	0.05	0.05	0.05	**0.12**	-0.03	**0.18**	0.00
5	0.09	0.10	**0.26**	**0.27**	0.07	**0.20**	**0.16**	0.09	-0.07	-0.06	0.04	0.04	0.13	0.13	0.12	**0.31**	-0.08	**0.44**	-0.01
10	0.18	0.20	**0.51**	**0.53**	0.14	**0.41**	**0.32**	0.18	-0.13	-0.12	0.07	0.08	0.25	0.25	0.25	**0.61**	-0.15	**0.88**	-0.01
Distance																			
model coefficient: Distance	**-0.190**	**-0.189**			**-0.179**	**-0.111**											**-0.659**		**-0.100**
Distance squared	**0.007**	**0.007**			**0.007**	**0.004**											**0.026**		**0.004**
effect from increase in distance, 1000 miles:																			
0.5	**-0.09**	**-0.09**			**-0.09**	**-0.05**											**-0.32**		**-0.05**
1	**-0.18**	**-0.18**			**-0.17**	**-0.11**											**-0.63**		**-0.10**
7.5	**-1.03**	**-1.02**			**-0.95**	**-0.60**											**-3.48**		**-0.53**
combined effects of trade and distance:																			
500 miles & trade share 10	0.09	0.11	**0.51**	**0.53**	0.05	**0.38**	**0.32**	0.18	-0.13	-0.12	0.07	0.08	0.25	0.25	0.25	**0.61**	**-0.47**	**0.88**	-0.06
7,500 miles & trade share 2	**-1.00**	**-0.98**	0.10	0.11	**-0.93**	**-0.52**	0.06	0.04	-0.03	-0.02	0.01	0.02	0.05	0.05	0.05	0.12	**-3.51**	0.18	**-0.53**
USADR																			
model coefficient	0.002		0.001		0.002	**0.005**	0.003		**0.006**		**0.005**		0.002		0.002	0.001	0.002	0.001	-0.002
effect from increase in % capitalization issued as ADR:																			
5	0.01		0.01		0.01	**0.02**	0.02		**0.03**		**0.03**		0.01		0.01	0.01	0.01	0.01	-0.01
20	0.04		0.02		0.04	**0.09**	0.06		**0.12**		**0.10**		0.04		0.04	0.02	0.04	0.02	-0.04
40	0.08		0.04		0.08	**0.18**	0.12		**0.24**		**0.20**		0.08		0.08	0.04	0.08	0.04	-0.08
UKLSE																			
model coefficient	**0.007**	**0.007**		**0.008**				**0.006**		**0.007**		**0.007**		0.003					
effect from increase in % capitalization listed on LSE:																			
5	**0.04**	**0.04**		**0.04**				**0.03**		**0.04**		**0.04**		0.01					
20	**0.14**	**0.14**		**0.16**				**0.12**		**0.14**		**0.14**		0.06					
40	**0.28**	**0.28**		**0.32**				**0.24**		**0.28**		**0.28**		0.11					
XLIST																			
model coefficient						0.005	**0.021**	**0.022**								0.002			
effect from increase in % capitalization listed on investor country exchange:																			
5						0.03	**0.11**	**0.11**								0.01			
20						0.10	**0.43**	**0.44**								0.04			
40						0.20	**0.85**	**0.88**								0.08			
Firm Concentration																			
model coefficient	0.157	0.040	**0.715**	**0.533**	**0.222**	**0.272**	**0.860**	**0.855**	**0.272**	**0.336**	**0.360**	**0.413**	**0.387**	**0.420**	**0.391**	**0.471**	0.105	**0.623**	**0.346**
effect from increase in fraction of capitalization in top 10 firms:																			
0.2	0.03	0.01	**0.14**	**0.11**	**0.04**	**0.05**	**0.17**	**0.17**	**0.05**	**0.07**	**0.07**	**0.08**	**0.08**	**0.08**	**0.08**	**0.09**	0.02	**0.12**	**0.07**
0.4	0.06	0.02	**0.29**	**0.21**	**0.09**	**0.11**	**0.34**	**0.34**	**0.11**	**0.13**	**0.14**	**0.17**	**0.15**	**0.17**	**0.16**	**0.19**	0.04	**0.25**	**0.14**
0.6	0.09	0.02	**0.43**	**0.32**	**0.13**	**0.16**	**0.52**	**0.51**	**0.16**	**0.20**	**0.22**	**0.25**	**0.23**	**0.25**	**0.23**	**0.28**	0.06	**0.37**	**0.21**
Beta																			
model coefficient	**-0.007**	**-0.009**	**-0.003**	**-0.004**	**-0.006**	**-0.005**	**-0.006**	**-0.009**	**-0.002**	**-0.004**	**-0.002**	**-0.003**	-0.002	-0.003	-0.002	-0.002	**-0.005**	**0.008**	**-0.006**
effect from increase in Beta:																			
1	**-0.01**	**-0.01**	0.00	0.00	**-0.01**	**-0.01**	**-0.01**	**-0.01**	0.00	0.00	0.00	0.00	0.00	0.00	0.00	0.00	**-0.01**	**0.01**	**-0.01**
5	**-0.04**	**-0.05**	**-0.02**	**-0.02**	**-0.03**	**-0.03**	**-0.03**	**-0.05**	**-0.01**	**-0.02**	**-0.01**	**-0.02**	-0.01	-0.02	-0.01	-0.01	**-0.03**	**0.04**	**-0.03**
15	**-0.11**	**-0.14**	**-0.05**	**-0.06**	**-0.09**	**-0.08**	**-0.09**	**-0.14**	**-0.03**	**-0.06**	**-0.03**	**-0.05**	-0.02	-0.05	-0.02	-0.02	**-0.08**	**0.12**	**-0.09**
Entries in bold are significant at the 10 percent confidence level																			
Mean of dependent variable: float-adjusted portfolio weight	0.454	0.454	0.453	0.453	0.454	0.583	0.647	0.647	0.579	0.579	0.297	0.297	0.294	0.294	0.304	0.323	0.681	0.681	0.248
R²	0.217	0.219	0.196	0.199	0.227	0.282	0.709	0.718	0.536	0.538	0.230	0.253	0.317	0.318	0.294	0.421	0.226	0.144	0.166
N	1285	1285	1287	1287	1285	556	174	174	300	300	293	293	220	220	180	144	220	220	343

Appendix 1

A Theoretical Framework

Martin and Rey (1999) devised a simple 2-country model with risk-averse agents, transaction costs in cross-border trade, and an endogenous number of assets that are imperfect substitutes. Their insight was to apply a gravity model from trade to international portfolio flows. This framework gives rise to significant demand and market size effects on asset prices. Others have extended their model - a recent example is Faruquee, Li and Yan (2004) - the discussion below largely summarizes this approach.

Consider an N-country world in which each country x has n_x identical agents who are risk-averse and immobile. In period 1, each agent h, $h \in \{1,....,n_x\}$, is endowed with i units of a freely traded good (the numeraire) and chooses to develop k_{hx} risky projects, shares of which return a dividend in the next period, d_{hx} in one of the T exogenously-determined and equally- likely states of the world. Agents can hold on to their projects or sell shares in them at price, p_{hx}. The market capitalization of all shares of the projects in country x is thus:

$$MC_x = \sum_{h=1}^{n_x} p_{hx} k_{hx}$$

And total world market capitalization is:

$$MC = \sum_{x=1}^{N} MC_x$$

It is assumed that the number of projects in the world, P, is less than T, the number of states, so that all risk cannot be diversified. There will be some states where no dividends are realized. If we assume that no agent duplicates another's project, then the total number of projects is:

$$P = \sum_{x=1}^{N} \sum_{h=1}^{n_x} k_{hx} < T$$

For simplicity, it is assumed that all risky projects in a given country have the same dividend, d_x. Each project is thus an Arrow-Debreu security with a payoff of d_x if x=t, $t \in \{1,....,T\}$ and no payoff when x≠t. Since different projects have returns in different states of nature, assets are imperfect substitutes and diversification can improve an individual's welfare. In period 1, each agent consumes and invests in projects. In addition to his income, i, he sells shares in his project and buys shares of other projects. Because all home assets have the same *ex ante* return, perfect competition should equalize the price of shares across a given countries' projects. Therefore, we assume $p_{hx} = p_x$ for all x, $x \in \{1,....,N\}$

When agents buy foreign securities, it is assumed that they bear a transaction cost, τ, which is specific to each country pair. This transaction cost can be thought of as a fee collected by financial intermediaries but it can also be seen as the information cost associated with dealing with a foreign entity. An individual in the xth country's purchase of securities from country y then would cost $p_y(1 + \tau_x^y)k_{hx}^y$. Cross-country dividend payments also are subject to this cost, a sharehold in country x, will receive only $(1-\tau_y^x)d_y$ per share in country y's projects. We employ the simplifying assumption that transaction costs are symmetric so that $\tau_x^y = \tau_y^x > 0$ if $x \neq y$, and $\tau_x^y = 0$, if $x = y$.

The budget constraint for a consumer h in the home country, x, is then:

$$c_{1,hx} + \sum_{y=1}^{N}(1+\tau_x^y)n_y p_y k_{hx}^y = i + p_x \sum_{y=1}^{N} k_y^{hx}$$

And assuming he or she maximizes the following utility where β is the discount factor and σ is the inverse of the degree of risk aversion:

$$\text{Max } U_{hx} = c_{1,hx} + \beta E[c_{2,hx}^{1-1/\sigma}/(1-1/\sigma)]$$

and that given the payoff structure of these economies:

$$E[c_{2,hx}^{1-1/\sigma}/(1-1/\sigma)] = 1/S\sum_{y=1}^{N}[n_y[(1-\tau_x^y)d_y k_{hx}^y]^{1-1/\sigma}(1-1/\sigma)]$$

Using the first order conditions, one can arrive at the following share demand equations:

$$k_{hx}^{hx} = (\beta/T)^\sigma d_x^{\sigma-1}/p_x^\sigma$$

$$k_{hx}^y = (\beta/T)^\sigma d_y^{\sigma-1}(1-\tau_x^y)^{\sigma-1}/[p_y(1+\tau_x^y)]^\sigma, y \neq hx$$

Market clearing conditions require that all the shares of a project sum to 1 or

$$\sum_{x=1}^{N} n_x k_{hx}^y = 1, y = 1\ldots\ldots N$$

And using the simplifying assumptions that projects in each country are homogenous and their shares are equally priced, we can rewrite each country's market capitalization as:

$$MC_x = \sum_{h=1}^{n_x} p_x k_{hx} = n_x p_{x,} x = 1\ldots\ldots N$$

Country x's holdings of country y's projects is then:

$$K_x^y = \sum_{h=1}^{n_x} p_y k_{hx}^y = n_y p_y n_x k_x^y, y \neq x$$

Rearranging terms:

$$K_x^y = (\beta/T)^\sigma MC_x MC_y [d_y(1-\tau_x^y)]/p_y]^{\sigma-1} /(1+\tau_x^y)^\sigma p_x p_y$$

Country x's holdings of country y's equities is positively related to both country x and y's market capitalization, and the return on country y's equities (d/p) given σ>1 some degree of risk aversion. In this case, x's equity holdings in y are negatively related to transaction costs and the number of states of nature. Country x's holdings of home securities simplifies to:

$$K_x^x = n_x(\beta/T)^\sigma (d_x/p_x)^{\sigma-1}$$

Then the share of country x's portfolio invested in country y is simply:

$$S_x^y = K_x^y / \sum_{y=1}^{N} K_x^y$$

and comparing this share with relative market capital, the relative weight of country y's equity in country x's portfolio is:

$$W_x^y = S_x^y /(MC_y/MC) = (\beta/T)^\sigma n_x(MC/\sum_{y=1}^{N} K_x^y)[(1-\tau_x^y)d_y/p_y]^{\sigma-1}/p_y(1+\tau_x^y)^\sigma$$

This equation can be linearized to arrive at a version of the equation estimated above where the weights depend positively on the size of a country, n_x, the returns (d/p), and a constant that represents a combination of the rate of discount, the number of states, and the size of the global market relative to the total domestic portfolio, and depends negatively on transaction costs (which may be related to information costs or fees or other impediments to trade) and the price of the destination country's equities.

Comparing two relative weights in two different countries:

$$W_x^y / W_x^z = [(1-\tau_x^y)d_y p_z /(1-\tau_x^z)d_z p_y]^{\sigma-1} /(p_z/p_y)[(1+\tau_x^z)/(1+\tau_x^y)]^\sigma$$

We find an expression that can be simplified to a simple ratio between relative transaction costs, dividends and prices.

$$w_x^{yz} = W_x^y / W_x^z = [(1-\tau_x^y)d_y /(1-\tau_x^z)d_z]^{\sigma-1}[p_z(1+\tau_x^z)/p_y(1+\tau_x^y)]^\sigma$$

Appendix 2

Results for Austria

Model A1 lists results from a model for Austria which ignores the outliers extreme overweights observed for the Czech Republic, Hungary, and Poland. In this specification, the only variables that enter significantly (at the 10 percent level) are BETA and a dummy for the euro area.

Models A2 and A3 demonstrate the importance of these outlier destinations: these destinations enter with highly significantly coefficients ranging in size from about 17 for Poland to nearly 70 for the Czech Republic. Once these outlier destinations are controlled for, we find that TRADE is also a significant explanatory variable for Austrian portfolio allocation; in terms of economic significance, the increase is marked: an increase in the share of trade with a given destination country from 2 to 10 percent raises the Austrian portfolio weight in that country from about .15 to between .7 and .8. USADR does not enter significantly in A2, nor does XLIST, but UKLSE enters at the 5 percent level in model A3. The coefficient on UKLSE suggests an important contribution from this variable as well: an increase in a country's market capitalization cross-listed in London from 0 to 40 percent raises the estimated portfolio weight in that country by about .7. FIRMCON enters significantly in both A2 and A3; the implied contribution from an increase in the market capitalization accounted for by the top 10 firms from .2 to .6 increases the estimated Austrian portfolio weight in that country by about .4 (in A2) and .5 (in A3). As we found for other euro-area countries, the dummy variable for euro area destination enters significantly (at the 10 percent level), and the dummy variable for Belgium-Luxembourg is very large and significant. The dummy variable for US destination enters with a negative but insignificant coefficient in both A2 and A3, suggesting that after accounting for the overweights observed in specific locations, U.S. equities are neither favored nor disfavored in Austrian portfolios relative to other foreign equities, and the relative weight placed on U.S. equities can be explained by trade shares, listing in London, and market concentration.

Appendix Table: Results for Austria

	A1		A2		A3	
CONSTANT	20.786		-0.514		-1.204	*
TRADETOT	-0.043		0.069	**	0.082	**
DISTANCE	-3.011		0.046		0.146	*
DISTSQR	0.128		-0.003		-0.007	*
MCAPGDP	-3.721		0.032		-0.125	
EQTYBOND	-0.379		-0.017	*	-0.005	
USADR	-0.127		0.002			
UKLSE					0.018	*
XLIST	0.078		0.004		-0.016	
FIRMCON	2.373		0.948	*	1.255	*
BETA	-0.259	+	-0.002		-0.001	
EURO	-7.699	+	0.583	+	0.511	+
BELUX	7.943		16.217	**	16.757	**
CZECH REPUBLIC			70.051	**	70.278	**
HUNGARY			22.603	**	22.959	**
POLAND			17.144	**	17.271	**
US	12.112		-0.196		-0.003	
N	44		44		44	
Adjusted R^2	0.1188		0.9975		0.999	
Mean of dependent variable	3.241		3.241		3.241	

** significant at 1 percent
* significant at 5 percent
+ significant at 10 percent

www.ingramcontent.com/pod-product-compliance
Lightning Source LLC
Chambersburg PA
CBHW080630290526
45790CB00007B/2995